COWS CAN BE PURPLE:
My Life and Art Therapy

by
Sadie E. (Tee) Dreikurs
Honorary Master of Arts in Counseling Psychology,
Honorary Doctor of Laws

Edited by:
Nancy Catlin, Ph.D.
Psychologist in private practice
Seattle, Washington

James W. Croake, Ph.D.
Professor
Psychiatry and Behavioral Sciences
School of Medicine
University of Washington
Seattle, Washington

ALFRED ADLER INSTITUTE
OF CHICAGO

Copyright © 1986 by Sadie E. (Tee) Dreikurs
Library of Congress Catalog Card Number 86-071654
Printed in the United States of America
ISBN 0-918560-32-2

All rights reserved. No part of this work may be reproduced
or transmitted in any form or by any means, electronic or
mechanical including photocopying, recording or by any information storage and retrieval system, without permission in
writing from the publisher.

Alfred Adler Institute of Chicago, Inc.
618 South Michigan Avenue, Chicago, Illinois 60605

Dedication

I herewith lovingly dedicate this book to my four grandchildren, Rodney, Beth, Bruce, and Linda Ferguson. When they were little children they'd say, "Grandma, why don't you write a book so you can be famous like Grandpa?" Here is my book, and it's dedicated to their desire for me to be "great like Grandpa."

THE AUTHOR

Acknowledgments

There are so many people to whom I want to express my gratitude. I have indeed been fortunate in having truly great people influence my life: Jane Addams of Hull-House, who trained me as a social worker; Blanche Maggioli, who introduced me to a life of painting; my friend Sam Greenburg, whose dearest wish was that I write this book so that other painters could benefit from it; my first husband, Leon Garland, who thought I was a great painter; and my second husband, Rudolf Dreikurs, who taught me to understand human behavior and enabled me to develop the art therapy I now use as an Individual Psychologist.

I wish to acknowledge with gratitude the contribution made by Dr. Nancy Catlin and Professor James Croake, when they inspired me to write this book. Actually, I could accuse them of sneaking up on me. They were visiting with me during an art therapy workshop in Vancouver and taped my responses to their questions about my childhood and my training in art. As they prodded me with questions about how all this fit in with my art therapy, and encouraged me to elaborate on what I do with groups, I realized that my techniques were deeply embedded in Adlerian theory, and writing them down might be of value to other clinicians. I had no intention of writing such a book, but Nancy and James convinced me that it could be done. They continued to tape our informal discussions and agreed to write up the material as my editors.

They could not have done this without their expertise in Adlerian psychology. They are both seasoned Adlerians and understood so well what I was trying to say in spite of my frequently clumsy manner of expressing myself. This book would never have been written without them.

I also want to express my appreciation to my dear son-in-law, Dr. George W. Linden, for reviewing the manuscript carefully and suggesting some important changes. He brought to it the clarification, closure and unification which were possible because of his unique perspective as a professional within the family.

Dr. Shulman graciously consented to write an introduction to this volume, but I wish also to acknowledge here his contribution to my professional growth. He gave me the opportunity to experiment with techniques and develop my own methods in art therapy at St. Joseph Hospital. I'm exceedingly grateful for his trust and confidence in me and in my ability to work with his patients.

Contents

Introduction

The inpatient psychiatric unit at St. Joseph Hospital in Chicago was probably the first such unit to be deliberately designed to the Individual Psychological theories of Alfred Adler. It was a newly opened unit in a large urban general hospital with a diverse patient population. Rudolf Dreikurs, my own teacher, had already shown me that Adler's ideas were applicable to all sorts of social groups – to school classrooms, to psychotherapy groups, to children's camps – why not to a psychiatric milieu?

The thought became father to the deed. Various specialists trained in Individual Psychology came to train nurses and other staff to create a cohesive group structure in which people helped each other to understand themselves and meet life more courageously. Patients learned to contribute to the welfare of each other, to help each other and learn from each other.

Among these specialists was Tee Dreikurs. She describes very well how she worked with the patients and staff. Since then she has gone on to continue her work and to teach others in different parts of the world.

Tee Dreikurs' description of *how* she does her work is clear and straightforward. From her description we can see that she creates a set of therapeutic experiences for the participants in her workshops. They become less inhibited, more spontaneous, more communicative, more cooperative, more sensitive to others, more group-minded and more aware of themselves. In her hands, painting became a powerful tool for understanding and encouraging others.

The story in this book develops as if the author were painting a picture. First comes the background, and then comes the spatial organization which brings us to the "golden circle" of the painting – the description of what Tee as therapist actually does. The story of her own personal development parallels the stories of participants experiencing themselves in art therapy workshops. She, too, looks at what she has learned from others; she creates her own contribution which she lovingly shares.

When I first talked to Rudolf Dreikurs about bringing Tee to the psychiatric unit at the hospital, I was thinking about the benefits to the patients themselves. I think Rudolf Dreikurs saw beyond me. He could see it as more than that – as a way of making a larger contribution to the social milieu in which we all live. Tee Dreikurs has been busy building more stately chambers for all of us.

B. H. Shulman, 1984

Preface

When Tee Dreikurs was born, she weighed slightly more than two pounds. For a child of such small birth weight to survive today is not unusual. Medical technology has made some miracles everyday events. But for a child of two pounds to survive in the more primitive medical world of 1900 was certainly unusual. It may not have been a miracle, but it was an exceptional event.

As the doctor was washing the newborn child, Tee's small hands reached out. She grabbed and maintained a firm grip on the rim of the ceramic bowl. "This kid will make it," said the doctor. "She's a fighter."

This kid did make it. And, as *Cows Can Be Purple* demonstrates, she grew into an exceptional woman. Tee Dreikurs *is* a fighter. But she is not a fighter of life nor of people. She is not a fighter *against*. She is a fighter *for*. Tee is a fighter for greater self-confidence. Tee is a fighter for creativity and contribution. Tee is a fighter for encouragement, cooperation, mutual respect and group solutions for individual and common problems. In short, she is a fighter for Social Equality.

This book was written in the hope that the unique methods developed by Sadie (Tee) Dreikurs, social worker, artist, and colleague of Rudolf Dreikurs, her husband, could be made available to other interested Adlerians and art therapists around the world. At Tee's request, this was written in the first person, using her own words and style, from taped interviews over the course of several years.

An autobiographical sketch is included in the beginning, because much of Tee's work in art therapy was intimately related to her own experience as a child, her studies in art and social work, and her relationships with significant others. Among these were her first husband, Leon Garland, an artist, and her second husband, the Adlerian psychiatrist Rudolf Dreikurs.

Because Rudolf was, in her words, Tee's "chief teacher," it was her choice to use quotations from his works, whenever

xi

possible, rather than from Adler's. As she explained in her inimitably charming way to her editors, "It may not be congruent with what other people think, but I choose to use his [Dreikurs'] formulations and the way he interpreted Adler's theory of Individual Psychology."

Although many of her acquaintances are not aware of it, Tee is an accomplished artist. She doesn't paint any longer, but her apartment walls are literally covered with her work and Leon's, and the editors are fortunate enough to have been given one of her pastels. She exhibited at the Art Institute of Chicago in the years between 1928 and 1941, and is a life member of the Institute since a one-man exhibition in honor of her first husband was presented in the newly opened Chicago room, after his death.

Tee has never become a member of the American Art Therapy Association, and for reasons she believes are not unlike those which prevented Rudolf Dreikurs from being initially accepted into the professional psychiatric community. After one of her first workshops, she was asked to submit a paper explaining her methods, for publication in the Association's journal. Her paper was returned to her six months later with the criticism that she was only using one theoretical frame of reference and was practicing more than just art therapy as they understood it. As Tee commented, "What I'm doing doesn't fit – any more than what Dreikurs did."

The reader should be cautioned that the methods and activities described in this text do not in themselves constitute a sufficient background in art therapy or Adlerian theory for a would-be therapist. This is not a training manual or a comprehensive treatise on either subject. It is, however, an attempt to convey some creative ideas about a novel approach to art therapy based on Adlerian psychology and at the same time share something about the creator, for whom there exists a great deal of affection and admiration among her many students, friends and colleagues around the world.

Tee advises those who would try her techniques that the three prime requisites for an art therapist are spontaneity, creativity, and the courage to be imperfect.* Additional skill in group dynamics, proficiency in painting and a sophistication in the arts are also of great value, as well as a thorough understanding of the Individual Psychology of Alfred Adler.**

The organizational structure of this text is designed to flow from an autobiographical sketch into the first two chapters describing her art therapy, which are both theoretical and practical. These chapters are followed by explanations of specific group projects, additional ideas and general recommendations with a presumed knowledge based on information gleaned from the preceding chapters and finally some suggestions for application of these methods in a variety of therapeutic settings. The book concludes with an editorial discussion of the timeliness and significance of "Cows Can Be Purple."

This book is not an autobiography. It is not a collection of wistful reminiscences. This book is not a history. It is not a chronicle of exquisite regrets. It is a useful book. A book that presents principles, techniques and strategies for Adlerian Art Therapy. And, ultimately, it is a book of theory. It presents in concrete working form a theory of psychology and a goal of mental health based on Social Interest. Although Tee may object, we believe that this book is ultimately philosophic. It presents us with a view of human brotherhood that we can all utilize to become more adequate human beings.

Nancy Catlin,
James W. Croake and
George W. Linden

---

*"The courage to be imperfect" is a phrase coined by Sofie Lazerfield, but it was Dreikurs who integrated the phrase into all of his work. It means to take the chance of making a mistake, to forthrightly attempt to solve the problems of living without the safe guarding propensity of self-deception. Dreikurs continually demonstrated the courage to be imperfect when he worked with patients. He never dodged the task and never predicted the outcome but would say when asked how he thought the therapy would go, "Let's try it and see how it goes."

**In North America the major training center is the Alfred Adler Institute of Chicago. Training can also be obtained, often in cooperation with the Chicago Institute, at the Alfred Adler Institute in Toronto, New York, Bowie State College, The British Columbia Society for Individual Psychology, The University of Oregon, Arizona State University, and many other colleges and universities in the United States. Throughout Europe and in Israel Adlerian Psychology training is available thanks mostly to the efforts of Rudolf Dreikurs who also founded the Institute in Chicago.

Part I

An Autobiographical Sketch

The Schwartzeh

The Purple Cow

My first grade teacher handed me a pattern for a cow. In those days, painting lessons consisted of tracing and filling in a pattern with color. I was a city person and had never seen a cow. Purple was a desirable color to me, so I filled in the pattern with purple. The teacher came by and said, "Cows are not purple. Cows are brown." She tore up my paper and gave me another with an outline on it, but I refused to do it. I had to stay after school and stand in the corner, but I would not fill in the drawing.

That was the end of my creative activity for many years, although I continued my preference for purple. I was a girl smashed between a beloved younger brother, who in those days wore blue, and a beautiful sister who wore pink, and if one combines pink and blue the result is purple. I was purple from the start. I even wanted my purple cow to be pretty like my sister and mischievous like my brother.

A Small Beginning

I was a tiny baby, only two-and-a-half pounds, and I hung on for dear life. The doctor said, as I was being bathed in a small basin, "Oh, she's a smart one. She's hanging on." The story goes that when my aunt brought her children in to see me as an infant, they ran out screaming "She's a devil!" because I was so ugly.

I had colic, I coughed, I was anemic and shallow-skinned, and later had to be kept out of school for an extended time because of bronchitis. I was skinny and my nickname was "Bones." I was so convinced of my own ugliness in childhood that later in life I was sure that no man would ever love me.

My sister, on the other hand, was radiantly beautiful with blond hair and rosy cheeks. She glowed with health and was my mother's helper, taking care of me, a puny little thing. My brother, five years younger, was the handsomest little fellow you could imagine.

1

I have a picture, taken when Charlotte was eight, I was six, and Charles was one. My sister standing there as big as life, sure of her prettiness, her blond hair all curls; my charming brother is the beautiful baby; and I am looking simply miserable, a thoroughly wretched little creature. I didn't feel pretty at all, although my mother had put my hair in rags so that I had corkscrew curls for the occasion. Looking at the picture now, I see that I was rather pretty, but at the time I was impressed with the fact that I was not beautiful.

I grew up with the idea that I was ugly and not really a white person. When people raved about Charlotte's beauty my mother would have compassion and ask, "But what's wrong with Sarale?" The answer was, "She's a schwarzeh," which means "She is the black one." I was also referred to as Japanese because I had slanty eyes, high cheekbones and straight black hair.

I became a problem to my parents because I refused to eat. When guests came to our home, my mother would say, "I don't know how this child survives. You will see. She doesn't eat a thing." Of course I obliged her by not eating.

Because I was sickly as a little girl, everyone took care of me. Mother made me take a nap as soon as I came home from school, and Charlotte would sew on buttons for me. I was sheltered completely. "Don't wash the dishes. You're too weak and you might break them. You must conserve your energy so that you can do your homework and go to school tomorrow."

In my old age I am still following the same pattern. People protect me right and left. Charlotte at 84 will call me up on a cold day and say, "Be sure to dress warmly."

As can be seen from these early experiences, I had already learned the values of companionship and rebellion. I had also experienced inferiority feelings directly. I did not think that I would ever be able to attain the beauty of my sister. Nor did I ever believe that I could grow to be as lovely as my mother.

My Parents

My family lived in back of my father's shop in Chicago and my mother helped him with the business. They had a very tempestuous relationship, because Mother was a rare beauty, 28 years younger than he, and he was horribly jealous of her. When he had to leave her alone in the shop, his only sense of security was the knowledge that women did the marketing rather than men. Otherwise, he would not have left her because he wouldn't trust her.

We children adored both of them except when they started to fight, and then we had very mixed feelings. If I thought Mother had started the fight, I hated her because she was scolding my dear father, but if I thought he was at fault, I hated him for distressing my beautiful mother.

Mother

We lived in a huge area behind the shop, with a private entrance. It was one square room with cubicles, blocked off with curtains, similar to a hospital ward. We had a black coal stove and a sink in a little area where all the equipment was used, including a wooden washtub which was pulled out every Friday after Mother had started preparing the Sabbath meal. She did everything very systematically.

First she would bake the traditional Sabbath braided egg bread which is called "challah." Then she started cooking the gefilte fish, chopping it up with onions and mixing in all the other ingredients. She cooked the chicken in a pot, and rendered the fat which she skimmed off. Later in life when I walked into that kitchen, all these odors came back to me, intermingled with the fragrance of Fels Naptha soap.

As a Sabbath meal was cooking, Mother would heat the water, fill the wooden washtub, and one after the other we would take our weekly bath. She scrubbed us properly until we were shining clean and ready for the Sabbath. Then she'd take the soap suds left from the last bath, get down on her hands and knees, and scrub the kitchen floor from end to end until it

3

was beautifully white. After this she hid herself and took her own bath, washing her long black hair in the Fels Naptha soap, which made it glisten like diamonds. When is was dry she wound it around her head and the Sabbath candles were lit.

Mother didn't have a proper shawl, so she'd take a white towel to cover her head and stand in front of the lighted candles. My strongest memory from childhood is the vision of her beauty, her sparkling black eyes and bright red cheeks from all her efforts, and her wonderful shiny black hair. All this was intermingled with the cooking smells. Mother was completely illiterate but repeated the words in literate fashion and blessed the candles.

Father

On Saturday morning we had a different routine. It was one of the few times Father had with his children. He sat in his huge wooden rocking chair, and my sister Charlotte and I would each sit on a knee while Charles, the baby of the family, stood on Father's feet. Then he'd rock back and forth in his chair while we took turns playing with his moustache. He'd try to bite our hands which produced peals of laughter, because he could never catch us. It was just great!

Finally we would settle down and he'd tell us stories of his days in Lithuania before he left at the age of 19. He painted very visual pictures with his story telling, as my brother and I did in later years. These wonderful stories which he wove were elaborated on at length and became exaggerated over the years. One example was the story of his great strength.

My father was a very strong man until he had an accident. He lived on his uncle's mill and helped with the packing of the flour and taking it to market. When the story was first told, the sack of flour weighed at least 50 pounds. He would put it over his shoulder and get it into the wagon with no trouble at all. After three years, the sack weighed 2,000 pounds, and he could still throw it over his shoulder with no trouble whatsoever.

He painted these verbal pictures for us and we could visualize the whole scene. My father had a strong influence on my imagination for I soon became able to see what he told me in words. When I visited Lithuania in 1929 I found

4

everything exactly as he'd described, even the tastes of the food my cousin served.

My paintings and the stories I tell are inextricably enmeshed in my cultural and Jewish background which I absorbed from my father. He painted pictures with his stories of the small shtetl (village) in Lithuania. They reflected the rituals and superstitions about spirits and demons which were born out of the Jewish communities in these countries, and for me they are a treasured gift. My father really wasn't cut out to be a businessman. He failed in business constantly. His meat market was not a success.

Chicago

Most of my recollections are of sights and smells and places, and not just social situations. Chicago, when I was four or five years old, was a picturesque city. The streets were made of stumps of trees with earth packed around them to keep them steady, the sidewalks were wooden, and there were only horse-drawn conveyances. Vendors came down the street clanging their bells and selling various items.

One was an Italian vendor who had a pretty cart with a fringed awning around it. He sold eight or nine flavors of shaved ice for a penny. You'd point to a flavor and he'd make a cone out of a newspaper, put the shaved ice in it and then add the flavor. This was a delicacy. I remember one time, just as I was about to put one in my mouth, a red fire engine drawn by six white horses with their tails up high came rattling down the street and stirred up all the dust, which settled on the cone, ruining my delight.

The ice man delivered ice on a wagon with his horse and we would follow along behind, picking up the bits of fallen ice and sucking on them. It was a great event. He'd cut a block of ice, put it in a dirty old sack which he'd throw over his shoulder. Since all the children would forget to empty the pan under the icebox, there were constant puddles in everybody's house.

Blanche

At the age of 11, on the first day of school in September, I met Blanche Maggioli. I stepped out of my middle child position in my own family and became part of her world. Everything Blanche wanted to do, I wanted to do. I escaped being sandwiched between my very capable, beautiful sister and my mischievous darling brother. Albeit, everybody continued to protect me and do things for me, and I continued to depend on someone to provide leadership and to take care of me. Later in life I had to change my role and become a caretaker for my husband, Leon Garland. That indicated my growing flexibility.

The Path to Hull-House

Blanche and I had a marvelous relationship. She had as much imagination as I, and was a very creative person. It was through her that I became interested in painting. On the day I met her, she had a music lesson after school at Hull-House, which was about a mile from where we lived, and I walked along with her. This walk to Hull-House became a source of joy – all the sounds, smells, and beautiful sights.

We walked through a small wooded square amidst the jungle of tenements, dubbed "Peanut Square" because the peanut vendors rested here during the day and exchanged stories while eating their lunch. The organ grinders also rested here and the monkeys would jump around and tip their hats when you gave them a penny.

After Peanut Square we entered an exclusively Italian neighborhood where vendors had their vegetables out in front of their stores. Each house had a row of green peppers and tomatoes drying on the window for making spaghetti during the winter. We could smell these pungent odors, savor the colors of the vegetables like confetti, and hear the neighbors shouting to one another. The streets were full of children playing. It was so different from my own neighborhood – a whole new world of sights, smells and sounds.

6

Chicago was not a unified city but a series of exotic ethnic neighborhoods. This environment helped me adjust to the international milieu of Jane Addams, and these early experiences shaped me so that later in life I found it easy to adapt to different countries, cultures and peoples. This was democracy in living.

The original Hull-House was a private mansion. Jane Addams founded it as a social settlement in 1889. In addition to the original Hull mansion, which, being made of brick, was one of the only buildings to survive the Chicago fire, Jane Addams had designed additions favoring the architecture of Toynbee Hall in London where she had received her inspiration. When I saw this marvelous place for the first time, there was a total of 13 buildings, and in the courtyard was the music school where we sat waiting for Blanche's lesson.

Art Lessons

We had a half hour to wait, and Blanche said, "Why don't we paint the geranium on the window?" So we did. Coincidentally on that day we had been painting in school and we each had with us a little tin with red, blue, and yellow watercolors, a pad, and a brush.* We were in the process of painting the geranium when Emily Edwards, a lovely tall young woman, came in and in a southern voice said, "Children, what are you doing here? You belong in the art class."

She took us in immediately and that was the end of Blanche's music lessons. We remained in the art classes from then on, and when we were 15, Jane Addams became interested in us after hearing from Emily that we were talented young girls. She obtained scholarships for us at the Art Institute. That was the beginning of my artistic career. Although I began to realize that I could paint, I never believed I really had much ability. I was only doing it because Blanche was, and it was part of our relationship. Later, experience and Leon helped me gain more confidence in my abilities.

Summer Camps

Two years later we went to Hull-House summer camp in Waukegan. We were fortunate enough to be given a room of

---

*By this time I was painting what the teacher told me to.

our own, because we were such close friends, instead of being in the dormitory with other girls. As is often true for me, I was struck by the physical surroundings of this place. There was a deep ravine outside our window, and it seemed to me as if we were on the precipice of a mountain. In later years I went back to look at it and realized that it was only a slight incline, but at the time it was a real mountain.

Even in our private room the nights were very cold. I respected Blanche's Catholicism and she respected my Judaism, so when she got on her knees on the cold floor the first night we were there, I said "In our religion we don't kneel and I might as well stay in bed under the covers and say my prayers." I didn't actually pray at all, because I had never done so as a child, but I accepted the idea that Blanche needed to pray.

This went on for the entire 14 days. I wondered why she prayed so long each night. By the time she finally got up, her knees were sore and she shivered from the cold. When we were adults I asked her, "Blanche, why did you pray so long? Did you have so many sins?" She replied, "I wasn't praying at all. I thought you were praying and I didn't want to interrupt you. I kept waiting for you to say 'I'm done praying. Good-night.'" In this way I learned the importance of social interaction and the strong influence of mutual respect.

Judaism and Christianity

Blanche and I really combined our religions. I went to confesson with her, and she'd go to Sabbath School with me. We did everything to please each other. My parents were quite worried that I would marry an Italian and they didn't like my going to Hull-House.

Planning Our Careers

We decided that as soon as we were old enough to leave home we would go to Rome to paint, and Blanche decided that we couldn't afford to have a love relationship with anyone because that would interfere with our plans.

It didn't happen like that at all. At age 18, Blanche bravely set off for New York City with a portfolio, to break into the commercial art field. She was a pretty, dainty young woman, and everywhere she went, men were interested in having a relationship with her but not in giving her a job. She became very discouraged and was about to leave New York when she met Walt Disney while walking down Fifth Avenue. Walt Disney had been in high school with us. He told Blanche to forget the commercial art business and go to Hollywood where she could work as a writer and illustrator for him in his new studio.

Blanche Went to Hollywood

She went and we parted. However, she still considered me a traitor when I announced my engagement to Leon Garland in 1927. Although she was a good friend of Leon's, she still felt that it was a betrayal. Tragically, when I sent her a wire informing her of Leon's death in 1941, I received one from her in reply, "I have just married." She was 38 years old before she ever married.

For awhile we did not communicate or see each other. After her husband died we resumed our relationship, although our paths have diverged somewhat over the years. The change in our life situations separated us temporarily and my extended travels did not include visits to the west coast. However, the death of my second spouse gave impetus to a resumed closeness with Blanche. We began to have telephone conversations and a more regular correspondence. We share our childhood memories now and we rekindle our feelings of being part of each other's lives. Friendship, like any relationship, needs to be worked on and cultivated. The rebirth and flowering of our deep friendship gave me a sense of recurrence, completeness and wholeness.

The Rebellious Child

I was never a good student, and I was disobedient as well. My very well behaved and efficient sister preceded me throughout school, and I was introduced as Charlotte Ellis' sister. She was described as an angel and I was the opposite. I was very rebellious, whispered to my neighbors when I wasn't supposed to, and did all sorts of devious things. Math was my worst subject. In no way did I believe I could solve problems on my own.

Charlotte, of course, was excellent in math. She was, in fact, the shining light of the school. Not only was she a good student, but she was so efficient in handiwork that she taught all the teachers and their friends how to crochet Irish lace, which was fashionable at that time and a very complicated craft. Charlotte's mathematical ability fitted her for the business world, where she became quite successful. My rebellion fitted me for the social world, for I could understand and easily relate to rebels, delinquents and misfits.

Financial Failure

By the time Charlotte was ready for high school, the ninth grade, Father's business had failed. Charlotte, therefore, went immediately to work as did I when I reached the ninth grade. We both took two-year business courses in night school which gave us grade 9 and grade 10. We had secretarial skills which allowed us to obtain fairly good jobs. Charlotte became quite competent as a secretary and earned $6.00 a week, which was considered a high salary. Even though I worked six and a half days each week, I completed the last two years of high school, which meant taking the general courses necessary for a diploma.

Our Financial Contribution

Everything my sister and I earned during high school and later on we gave to our parents for the general welfare of the family. We were given streetcar fare and lunch money if it was not possible to take a sandwich, but no other spending money. Charlotte and I went without lunch for several years and saved the money so that we could each have a season ticket to the opera.

We had three blouses and two skirts between us, so the blouses had to be washed every night. We wore the same size blouse, but I grew to be taller than Charlotte, so for awhile she had to wear my cast-off clothes and I got all the new ones. It was a sad time for her.

Finances Limit Formal Training

I had a very brief period of study at The Art Institute of Chicago when I was 15. Through the scholarship which Jane Addams had provided I attended after school for a few months until my father's business failed. Then I was forced to discontinue my studies and forfeit the scholarship.

Miss Addams, who knew me quite well, was discouraged that I had to give up my scholarship, and requested that I come and work at Hull-House in the children's art school. I didn't get paid for that, but she managed to give me a salary for checking out the trays for lunch and dinner at the cafeteria. I also had a job as a clerk in a mail order house, performing the kind of menial tasks assigned to untrained personnel.

At about age 17 or 18 I started to do some quasi-social work. In addition to clerical jobs and checking trays at Hull-House, I visited families in the neighborhood to find out who needed help, especially at Christmas time.

I continued during the next several years to study art at Hull-House with Ennella Benedict, who was a fine teacher and also an instructor at the Art Institute. I learned early that life could be difficult and to be a diligent worker. The only place that "success" comes before "work" is in a dictionary.

Free Travel

When the First World War broke out there was a great need for women to work. I was able to get another clerical job with the American Railway Express which I had for about two years. This opened up a whole world to me. We had free transportation, and I started to travel all over the country. I visited a favorite aunt, uncle and cousins in Baltimore. I went to New York. Sometimes I'd take a pass anywhere just for the train ride. This wanderlust fitted me for my travels in later years.

Leon

When I met Leon Garland, who was later to be my husband, I must have been about 21 or 22. After I was forced to sacrifice my scholarship at the Art Institute, I gave up on painting for awhile, but finally went back to it when Bill, whom I had known as a child in art class, urged me to join the group that was painting together at Hull-House. I became interested in Batik and began to study it with Leon, who was volunteering his services as the instructor at Hull-House.

Our group painted on Saturday afternoons and Sundays because we all had jobs during the week. Ennella Benedict was our mentor. Although she was quite advanced in years by then and frankly stated that she knew very little about cubism, the newfangled modern art form, she was willing to have us experiment with it to see what we could do.

A Romantic Beginning

Bill, a fellow student, was half-heartedly courting me at the time. He decided to go to Paris to study and, being the considerate person he was, asked Leon to take care of me and be my escort while he was gone. Leon proceeded to court me very arduously but assumed the arrangement could only be temporary.

In the meantime Bill met the girl who would become his present wife in Paris. They began to date. They became quite close, so that when they returned together, Leon felt free to continue dating me. He would call during the week and say, "I have two tickets for the opera Saturday night. Would you come with me?" One night at the opera he kept staring at me instead of watching the stage. I asked, "What are you doing?" "You're so beautiful," he said. "Stop it. I'm not beautiful," I replied. He was the first man to think I was beautiful.

Marriage

Leon and I also went sketching every Sunday, in Lemont, Illinois. One day he said to me, "Why are we pretending this

12

way? I love you very much. Why don't we get married?" I said, "Why not?" Our wedding announcements said, "Please don't send us presents. If you want to give us a gift, send money, because we plan to go to Europe to study art." We started our savings with this nest egg.

We were married in 1927, at Hull-House. I was 27, and he was 31. Jane Addams gave us our wedding party, and we moved in. All the residents had to volunteer their services, so Leon continued to teach metal and Batik and I was in charge of the children's art department, as Miss Benedict's assistant.

Life Together at Hull-House

Leon was a very shy person and was ill at ease the first time we ate dinner together with all the residents at Hull-House because he had to sit beside Jane Addams and didn't know how to behave. She put him at ease and had him talking in a very short time.

Jane Addams was vey skillful in putting others at ease. One of her methods was to adopt the table manners of the guest. I remember an Italian visitor who ate his lettuce with his hands. Jane Addams immediately picked up her own lettuce with her hands.

We had very little furniture when we moved into Hull-House. Our first Sunday morning we were sleeping in late with our two cots pushed together in the middle of the studio, when there was a gentle knock at the door. It was Jane Addams. Leon was petrified, God forbid, Jane Addams would see that we slept together. He ran and hid in the bathroom. Miss Addams came in and said, "I came to see what furniture you need. Please get dressed and let's see what we can find." We went from one place to another and she'd tell people, "Oh, you don't need this corner cupboard. The Garlands can use it." She furnished our whole place.

Before she left our apartment she looked around and said, "Let's go into the bathroom and see how it is equipped." I said, "I'm sorry, Miss Addams, but I have a man hiding in there." Of course she knew it was Leon.

During the time we lived at Hull-House, from 1927 until his death in 1941, Leon became one of her most valuable and trusted advisors in regard to decoration or art. During the WPA and the youth projects, he was in charge of the decoration

13

of all 13 buildings. He directed the mixing of colors, designed interiors, and had the whole theater redecorated.

Preparation for an International Perspective

In addition to the Italian visitor who ate lettuce with his hands, we had many guests from foreign countries at Hull-House. Jane Addams prepared me for feeling at home internationally. One night we entertained a Japanese lady in her traditional costume who was a delight to behold. She spoke to us at length about her country. I remember distinctly her contradictory words about peace. She said, "My dear friends, Japan is a peace loving nation. If the rest of the world will give her what she wants, she'll never fight."

A man from the neighborhood was there the same night to speak to us. As the youngest matron of Hull-House I was head of one of the tables. Out of the corner of my eye I watched Jane Addams who was carefully observing the table manners of both guests. She did not proceed to eat until they did, and made them feel completely comfortable by doing exactly what they did. It made a terrific impact on me. This ability to put oneself in the place of the other—to see, hear, feel and behave as the other on the basis of equality—later became a basic principle of my art therapy methods.

Painting in France and Germany

Andre L'Hote

Two years after Leon and I were married, we went to Europe to study painting. We started to study first with Fernand Leger in Paris, but his type of painting did not appeal to us. During this time we met a fellow student at lunch who said she'd found a great school, with Andre L'Hote, and she literally dragged us there.

Andre L'Hote was a fascinating instructor. Studying with him was the richest art experience of my life, and I learned more about technique from him than from any other teacher. He made the history of art more vital to me than any course on the subject, because of his unique methods. He carried with him a huge portfolio of reproductions. He'd look at our paintings and say, for example, "You seem to be painting in the style of El Greco." Then he'd thumb through the portfolio, find an El Greco, give us a history of how and why El Greco painted the way he did, and show us where the person was not quite living up to this tradition. He did this with any painter whom he thought influenced us. We also learned a great deal about the history of art from visiting the major museums all over Europe.

Art students at that time traditionally spent hours and hours copying paintings at the Louvre and drawing for hours before ever painting. Andre L'Hote dispensed with all this. He said, "You don't have to know how to draw or paint—just do it." This appeal to spontaneity and trust in the creativity of the individual later became part of my art therapy approach.

Andre L'Hote was a nonconformist in many ways. While he was recognized as an able painter, he refused to become a member of any gallery or have his own agent. He felt that if a studio sold one of his paintings and became rich because of it, he'd be forced to continue painting in the same way and his creativity would be restricted.

He was also a rebel in the way he taught us. He had four studios in operation simultaneously, with a total of about 100

15

students. He would set up a subject in each one – a still life, group of nudes, a clothed model, a single nude – and we would choose what we wanted to paint. Our instructions were as follows. "Make a spontaneous sketch from your immediate emotional response to the subject, and then put it aside. Make another sketch which will be a plan for your composition and which should reflect what I've taught you about dynamic symmetry. Make a third sketch putting in the petite decorations, or details. Then I want you to make a color sketch of everything. When this is done, put all the sketches aside and paint."

We painted by ourselves all week, and at the end of the week he would come to evaluate our work. We had to put our paintings around on the walls so he couldn't identify the painter. Since he had a pronounced weakness for pretty ladies, he didn't want this to influence him, but after awhile, of course, he began to recognize what we did. *"Le petit menage"* (the small household) was his name for Leon and me and our painting. As he looked at the paintings we'd done he would say, "While you are with me, paint as I paint. After you leave, forget what you learned, and paint as you want."

To Berlin

We stayed in Paris until just before the new year when Leon decided he wanted to study commercial art in Berlin, because he wanted to have a way of earning a living. We visited Lithuania where my parents were born, studied in Berlin for six months and once again returned to Andre L'Hote, toured southern France, and took part in L'Hote's summer school in Mirmande, where many of the paintings now in my house were painted, before coming home.

In Berlin I was not a student, although I was allowed to use the studio at the Erdmann Schule, and wanted to establish myself as a painter in the opinion of the instructors. This was a difficult time for me, because, while the students liked what I was doing, they were critical of the fact that my work had a French flavor to it. I was both a Jewess and an American, and they were anti-American, anti-French, and especially anti-Jewish. Here I learned to deal with discrimination and hostility.

16

Career in Social Work   Oct,

We returned to Chicago in 1930, at the height of the depression. I was coopted by the United Charities of Chicago, and my social work career began. They were so short of social workers during the depression that agencies accepted anyone who had studied with Jane Addams as an officially trained social worker. I worked first for United Charities, then for the Cook County Bureau of Public Welfare, and then went to work full time for Hull-House as a social worker. I became a case consultant. After the School of Social Service Administration was founded at the University of Chicago by Sofenispa Breckenridge and Grace Abbott, who had obtained their experience in association with Jane Addams while residents at Hull-House, volunteers who had trained with Jane Adams were no longer eligible for professional jobs. One had to study at this school and get a degree before being accepted as a social worker.

Leon's Heart Attack

Leon had his first heart attack when he was 33 and we were students together in Paris. We had gone to a theater and were standing because we couldn't afford to pay for seats. He excused himself and disappeared for a long while. I looked for him but couldn't find him. Finally I sent a man into the men's room. He was there and had collapsed.

Back in Chicago

After Leon's massive heart attack in 1934, the doctors insisted that he drastically limit his activities. In fact, they didn't know how he had survived the attack. For the next seven years, until the last year of his life, Leon was only up for a few hours of the day; otherwise he was in bed resting. I had to learn to become a caretaker.

This was difficult for him because he felt that he was putting a burden on me which rightfully should be his. We had previously done all the household chores together since both of us worked and we couldn't afford help. When he was ill, Leon couldn't do his share, but I don't think he ever really stopped coddling and protecting me. Although I continued to work and he didn't have to support me financially, he was always tender, caring, and very concerned about me. Even when he was sick, he helped me with my overwhelming fear of losing him, or of becoming ill myself so that I couldn't support us or take care of him.

I was the center of Leon's universe and there were no limits to his confidence in me. He filled me with a sense of "You can do it if you want to," and dispelled the perception I had of myself as the ugly middle child who had no place in my family. I highly valued this training in encouragement.

Leon thought I was very beautiful, and I was more inclined to take him seriously than the others who told me this, because I admired him as a painter and valued his sense of beauty. When he'd look at me admiringly, or ask me to pose for him — usually my face or hands — I'd think, "He's not just saying that to make me feel good. He really believes I'm beautiful." Sometimes I almost believed it myself.

Pampered by Leon

Because of his confidence in me, Leon contributed much to my development as an artist, but in other areas he tended to pamper me by fighting for me rather than encouraging me to fight my own battles. He took the same role as my brother,

18

and later Blanche, who were rebellious and willing to fight for me when I didn't have the courage. If I didn't like something that had happened, Leon either wrote a letter or spoke up to smooth the way for me, or express what I did not dare.

There were occasions during these seven years when he could do a little work at home, such as creating designs for fabrics which could then be sold. As a full-time social worker I now lacked confidence in myself as an artist, and did not want to compete with the one thing Leon had left which was strictly his own. I reduced the amount of painting I did and became a Sunday painter. Heaven forbid if someone were to say, "We like her work more than Leon's!" This would have been unacceptable to me.

On Sunday afternoons I'd put on some music and paint for half a day. The music distracted me from other thoughts and helped me relax so that I could get back into a receptive mood for painting. My last painting was a semi-abstract, a small one that I called "Beethoven's Fifth," which I did while listening to the music. The idea of using music in art therapy actualy originated with this experience.

Leon changed doctors in 1940, a year before he died, and the new doctor said he should be out doing more. He felt so liberated that he went on two sketching tours. We both went to Wisconsin and then he went by himself to Gloucester, Massachusetts, where he painted beautiful things.

Leon Dies and I Stop Painting

One month after Gloucester he died, and I stopped painting completely. There was no one to paint with, or for, so my painting career was over. I didn't touch paints again until the '50s when Rudolf Dreikurs twisted my arm and I did a few charcoal and pastel portraits, but nothing after that.

Actually, I never did think of myself as an artist in spite of Leon's faith in me. After my discouraging experience in first grade when the teacher admonished me with "Cows are not purple—they're brown," I continued to have the idea that art was something I could never do.

I was quite amazed when people admired something I'd done. In fact, I was astounded when I got the scholarship to the Art Institute. I felt that I'd received it only because I

19

was Blanche's friend and Miss Addams and Miss Edwards knew they couldn't separate us.

Doubted Talent

I recall going to an exhibition at the Art Institute one day and joining a tour led by Dudley Crafts-Watson, who explained the artists and their work to the tourists. He came to a painting of mine of St. Tropez, which was on display there, and started to analyze it. He saw things in it that I hadn't even intended or was aware that I had put into it, and made this statement: "You haven't seen too many of Sadie Garland's paintings, but you watch that lady in the future, because she's going to make a mark for herself." I looked around in disbelief and thought, "Blanche isn't here. Why is he saying this?"

Another time Andre L'Hote commented that something I had done was an example of excellent painting. I was sure that he was saying this because he thought I was an attractive woman, and that there was no truth in it. The students in Paris would occasionally say that Madame Garland was a better painter than Leon, and I would be furious. I knew this could not be true, since I was only studying art because I was his wife and wanted to paint with him.

Although I never really valued what I did as a painter, I thoroughly enjoyed the process. I didn't consider that I had any talent, but painting gave me a great sense of doing something unusual. I was continually surprised by the product and would think, "Did I really do this?" Even now in retrospect, I have a certain detachment about my paintings as I look at them. I don't believe that I did them. Some other person must have done them and signed my name. It's not possible that I produced them. Perhaps because I never really believed in myself as a painter, I have derived more satisfaction from my contributions as an art therapist than as an artist.

The Beginning of Art Therapy

My career as an art therapist began at Hull-House in the mid-'30's, when my primitive need for survival saved me from a potentially disastrous situation. At that time I was employed as the director of community services and case consultant, but I was also in charge of the children's art department as a volunteer. I had been teaching art in the regular program there for a few years, during which time the neighborhood around Hull-House began to change.

Greek Residents

There was a group of Greek men without families living in a limited area within the Italian neighborhood who had never presented much of a problem. They worked, and spent their evenings in the coffee shops, smoking and playing Greek table games and cards, and occasionally having belly dancers come to perform for them. They typically sent their money back to Greece and eventually returned there to live. However, there was an upheaval in Greece in the mid-'30s and they began to bring their families over here.

Italian Rivals

Soon one whole area of Blue Island Avenue and Halsted Street was occupied by Greek families, and the children began to encroach on the territory of the Italian boys who would have nothing to do with them. The fights and stabbings became quite vicious. Many of the offenders were apprehended and sent away to a reform school or the juvenile detention home. Some were put on probation but there was no attempt at rehabilitation. The probation officers decided what to do with the boys, and most of them believed that if one could get the boys off the streets they'd become as pure as the driven snow. Of course they had to go somewhere, and Hull-House, with its recreational program, was the most convenient place. Amongst other activities it had a theater, a music program, a boys' club, and my art program. So you can guess what happened. I had these delinquent boys dumped in my lap and was told to take care of them.

Art for Delinquents

One decision was whether or not to integrate these acting-out delinquents with the well-behaved children who were already part of the regular program. With no experience in art therapy, let alone application with delinquents, we decided to put all of the children in one group. I had no experience in this whatsoever, and indeed, none of the social workers or group workers in those days knew how to deal with disruptive youth in a group. However, I decided to try getting them to paint and see what happened. I thought if I could teach them some skills in art the behavior might improve.

Picture two red brick buildings four stories high, with an alley between them. The art school was at the end of one of the buildings, in a huge room. When it was time for the painting class, two policemen were posted at the entrance. We opened the doors and the children ran in like sheep, pushing each other, until the room was filled. Then the doors were closed and the class began.

Where to Begin

At first everything went smoothly because they had to prepare the materials. Then they painted for a few minutes, but soon they began pushing each other around, egged on by their leaders. They got into fights, kicked each other under the tables, threw paint, and dumped over jars. Frankly, I didn't know what to do at this point. Should I give up and send them all out?

Coincidentally there was a roll of yellow wrapping paper left in the room, and I had an idea. Why not spread it all on the walls and get these adolescents out of the chairs where they wouldn't stay anyway, and have them paint standing up so that their activity might serve some constructive purpose?

Group Dynamics

I had spotted the gang leaders and I put one in charge of each wall. I merely announced that those who wished to work with Tony, Mike or Frank could go to that particular wall. I said, "This is your business. I'm not going to pay any attention to what happens. It's up to you to do what you want. If it doesn't work, we'll have to stop, but let's see if you can do something together with these three in charge."

When all the delinquents and regular students flocked to them, the three boys became constructive leaders. They talked over what they wanted to do and divided up the responsibilities.

An amusing incident remains in my memory and serves to illustrate the group behavior. There was one Italian boy whose nickname was Subby. He wore this name as if it were a badge of honor, although it referred to subnormal. To him, being called Subby was a great achievement. Mike said to him, "Subby, I know you can't do anything. I'll draw a cloud, and you fill it in with white." It was almost a case of the blind leading the blind. Yet Mike and Subby helped each other and taught me the positive importance and power of belonging.

Those in each group helped each other and cooperated, as they decided who was going to paint what. I would hear someone say, "I want to make this man run but I don't know how. Who can show me?" In this way they all became part of a group.

The leadership was complex and combined a rather loose democratic approach with an absolute autocratic rule. When a leader dictated what a group member should do, there was never any disagreement. The deviant youth were completely integrated with the regular ones without any harassment. It is ironic that this Greek/Italian conflict would sow the seeds of a future career. Many years later, after I had developed my methods of art therapy, I used them with the female inmates of a Greek prison. The fact that I had begun with Greek delinquents and ended with Greek felons and could help both groups gave me a sense of completion and wholeness, as if I had come full circle.

Beautiful Murals with Minimal Structure

This form of group painting continued over the next few years. I did structure the activity to some extent, but not to the degree or in the same way that I now do in the art therapy mural project. For example, in those days I would say to the boys, "Think of something that happened during the day or during the past week, and paint a picture of it in any way you choose." They'd talk over what they wanted to paint, and at one point they painted the Ohio flood for days on end. They

23

had seen pictures of it in the newspapers and translated these into paintings.

Their murals were of great beauty. I recall that for several years the murals were exhibited at Christmas time and were greatly admired by many people.

Success Born of Desperation

This mural painting, which was the origin of my art therapy with groups, was completely sparked by a primitive need to survive a desperate situation. I was responsible for this impossible project and didn't know what to do. I reacted spontaneously, feeling as if I were jumping into the water and might not come to the surface again. Fortunately, without consciously thinking about a solution, my creativity, or instinctual being, took over and served me well. I saw the roll of paper and a group of kids who were about to kill each other, and I went into action.

Even the idea of bringing in the gang leaders as my allies and letting them take over was a spontaneous response, arising from my perception of their strength in comparison to my own weakness. I had never even heard of doing this during my social work training. At that time I had not met Rudolf Dreikurs, but this was exactly what he would have done in the same situation. He knew that negative leaders could become positive ones.

Rudolf Dreikurs

The Need for More Understanding

I continued to do the group painting with adolescents for two or three years before meeting Rudolf and beginning my studies with him in 1938. I developed new techniques but was floundering in regard to a psychological understanding and approach to the group process. I knew I had to learn something more about how to help these young people, who were still getting into trouble when they weren't at Hull-House.

I discussed this problem at a meeting of social workers assigned to the many social settlements in the city. Elizabeth Baker, of Abraham Lincoln Center, which was trying to integrate Blacks and Whites, suggested that I come to a class being conducted by "a little Viennese professor."

The Professor Attacks

I hesitated to commit myself to this because Leon was recuperating from a heart attack and I didn't like to leave him alone all evening, but I thought I'd give it a try. I arrived a little late and heard this booming voice as I started to enter. "Social workers! What do they know about children? They collect facts, facts, facts, and all they have is factophilia, but do they understand the child? No!"

I was quite offended and had not come to be insulted, so I turned and started to walk out. Dr. Dreikurs spotted me and said, "Oh, come in, come in." Of course I came in then and sat down. After his tirade against social workers and the psychoanalytic method, he analyzed a case and I was fascinated.

However, when I returned home that evening I decided not to go to the class again. What he did was interesting but I didn't like the way he abused social workers and psychoanalysis. At that time I was taking a course with Franz Alexander and Karen Horney, and his attitude did not set well.

The next day Betty Baker called. When she heard my reaction to Rudolf Dreikurs, she said, "You're unfair. Come and try it again." I went another time, and during this session he analyzed a case, sentence by sentence – something I have since learned to do and have taught at the Rudolf Dreikurs International Summer Institute.

Dreikurs the Man

That night Dr. Dreikurs asked me to read a case history for his presentation, and I completely froze. I was trembling and could not utter a word. I didn't know what he was expecting, and I was terribly afraid to make the wrong guess. He excused me, but as we were leaving to go home he asked where I lived. When he discovered that he had to go in the same direction, he asked if he could come along with me. I really didn't want him to but we had to take the same streetcar anyway. As we were approaching Hull-House he asked me to have some coffee with him. I said, "I'm sorry but I have a sick husband and I really want to go home. I can't take the time to have coffee."

He answered, "I'll get off when you do and take the next streetcar," which he did. At the corner was a small Mexican coffeehouse, and he said, "It won't hurt to spend a few more minutes and just have a cup of coffee." He could sense that I was still frightened and wasn't relating to him at all.

I went in to the coffeehouse with him. The moment we started to sip our coffee he spied a pinball machine, whereupon he got up, walked over to it and began to play. I really was furious! No man had ever treated me that way, not even my husband. How could he offend my majesty and pay attention to the pinball machine after I was sacrificing so much to have a cup of coffee with him! I went over to him, said "Good night, Dr. Dreikurs," and walked out of the shop.

As I crossed the street I thought, "How stupid can I be? Why am I so afraid? This is just a little boy having a good time with a pinball machine." I laughed at my fear of him, and from then on did not take offense at anything. I thought of him as a soft, gentle human being who can enjoy pinball machines in spite of the great elegance of his knowledge and all he had to offer.

When I got home I apologized to Leon for being late and told him what had happened. Leon was intrigued with my description of Dreikurs and expressed a desire to meet him.

26

The next day at breakfast I was talking with Charlotte Carr, who had become the head resident of Hull-House after Miss Addams' death. When I told her about Dreikurs she was fascinated and suggested that he be invited as guest speaker at the next Federation of Settlements meeting which was to be held at Hull-House. When he came, he gave his usual case analysis. Everyone was charmed, and Charlotte was so delighted with him that she offered him an apartment at Hull-House that was vacant at the time.

Dreikurs Comes to Hull House

Immediately after his talk she confronted him with "Where do you live? Do you have a family?"

"Yes, I have a sister and a daugther living with me, and my son's in the army."

"How would you like to live here? You'd be charged a nominal rate but would be expected to make a contribution. You could be Sadie's consultant."

Rudolf accepted the invitation and came to live at Hull-House.

I invited him, his sister Bertha, and his daughter Eva to brunch on the first Sunday after they moved in. Leon was in the midst of painting, experimenting with under-painting and over-glazing paintings of the old masters. This was very strange to Rudolf, who had never seen anything like it. It looked as if all the figures were in brown shades, so Rudolf proceeded to criticize Leon's work. Leon responded at the onset by saying, "Dr. Dreikurs, I'm not going to tell you how to do your job. Please don't tell me how to do mine."

Thereafter they became the closest of friends. Leon admired Rudolf's skills, and Rudolf began to spend a great deal of time with the two of us on a social basis.

Working with Dreikurs

Rudolf and I worked together closely for about a year before Leon died. He opened a child guidance center at Hull-House too, and I went to the Abraham Lincoln Center with him as his social worker. Leon didn't seem to mind that I was spending more evenings working because I'd get some time off during the day.

About this time there was a struggle going on at Hull-House between Charlotte Carr and some of the old timers who were vying for leadership. A crisis evolved when some wanted to fire a whole group of the staff who were trying to help the Japanese resettle. It was a labor/race issue. Rudolf was guiding us all in dealing with this situation, and Leon illustrated for the staff in posters what was going on in the verbal battle. Everyone was delighted by the posters, which fortified our beliefs, and Leon loved to be involved, since he was also a fighter. The conflict became so intense that Charlotte's leadership was threatened and she eventually resigned. I became chairperson of a committee of five who functioned as the director.

Rudolf Responds to Leon's Death

In the midst of this struggle, in November, 1941, Leon died. It was a bad time in my life. Rudolf stepped in, to help me in my grief, and all of us during the crisis situation at Hull-House.

His tenderness during this period was wonderful. No matter what he'd been doing during the evening, or where he'd been, he'd tap at my door when he was through, even if it was eleven o'clock. I lived then in a penthouse studio at the top of one of the buildings. He'd bring a thermos of coffee and all sorts of beat-up stale cake he'd found in the house. We'd have coffee together and talk over all the activities. I never had therapy with him, but I could ask him anything about myself or how I was feeling.

One example was the situation that occurred about one month after Leon died, when there were five men courting me. I felt humiliated because I couldn't understand why they were pursuing me so soon after he had died. I felt I must be walking around like a bitch in heat.

Rudolf said, "It's very obvious. These are all men who knew you before Leon died. They knew of your relationship with Leon and that you had a marvelous marriage. They're interested in you because they know you're a great marriage prospect." Never once did I think *he* was a marriage prospect, and at the time I don't think he thought so either.

Eva Dreikurs

Soon after this, Rudolf came to my desk to ask a favor. "I have to be gone all evening. Bertha won't be home, and Eva will be all alone. If you'd be willing to stay and have supper with her, there's enough leftover food, and she'll warm up everything."

Eva was about 13 years old. She set the table and chattered away. As we sat down, she said, "Mrs. Garland, if you have any idea of marrying my father, you'd better be on the good side of me."

I replied, "Eva Dreikurs, I have no idea of marrying your father, and there's no reason for me to be on the good side with you. Your father just asked me to come and have supper with you, and I am perfectly willing to do that." This was my first contact with Eva after Leon died, and she was clearly worried that another queen bee might step in and replace her.

Rudolf as Suitor

Rudolf and I worked very well together. He'd invite me to listen to chamber music with him, and I got to know more of his friends, including Joseph Meiers and Ellie Redwin. I also became better acquainted with Bertha and established a close friendship with Rudolf's son, Eric, when he came home on furloughs.

One evening Rudolf asked me to go to a tavern for a drink. I ordered liquor and he ordered milk. He had been the founder of an anti-liquor league in Vienna and was adamantly against alcohol at the time.

The bartender said, "We don't serve milk."

"That's unfortunate," said Rudolf. "Send out for some." They did and he drank his milk while I had liquor.

He said to me, "You know Mrs. Garland, I don't know much about you. Why don't you tell me a bit about yourself? Tell me about your family constellation."

I told him about Charlotte and about how I'd grown up with the idea that I was ugly. He responded by saying, "You're quite right. You're really not very attractive. You're not a pretty woman."

It wasn't until two years after our marriage, when he commented one night on how beautiful I was, that I found out that he'd been teasing.

29

"What made you change your mind?" I asked. "You told me I wasn't good looking at all."

Rudolf was shocked. "Did you believe I meant that?"

"Of course I believed it. I thought 'even he doesn't think I'm pretty.'"

I still don't believe he thought I was very good looking. He admired many of my qualities, and I had high cheekbones and a face like his first wife and his girlfriend in Vienna, but they were much better looking than I.

I suppose I should have known that he was kidding me, and I probably would have if my own conviction of my ugliness had not been so entrenched. It was typical of Rudolf to tease me. If I'd ask, "Why did you marry me?" he'd reply, "For your money." I had only a $1,500 insurance policy from Leon, which we used to produce a portfolio of Leon's reproductions in order to create a reputation for him as a painter. Rudolf taught me that tension is always easier to take when it is clothed in humor.

Rudolf's Guidance

The Camp for Crippled Children

About two years after Rudolf came to Hull House, the bitterness and conflict within the large staff became so great that the Dreikurs' family moved out, and shortly thereafter I resigned. It was time for me to have another job, but first I thought I'd take a long vacation and go to the mountains to catch my breath.

As I was about to leave, a telephone call came through from the head of the Council of Social Agencies, Lucy T. Carner. She said, "I want you to get on a train for Burlington, Wisconsin, and look into the situation at a camp there for crippled children. I can't think of anyone but you who might be able to rescue that camp right now. The director, who is herself a crippled person and adored by all the children, has just left them all there and gone home after pandemonium broke out during a rainstorm the first night she was in camp. Now the question is whether to send these children home or try to find another director who can step in immediately."

I have never worked with handicapped children before, nor had I ever been in charge of a camp. Indeed, I didn't even want the job. What I really wanted to do was go away and rest. However, I went to look at the camp, to size up the situation.

Only one-fourth of the children were ambulatory. The rest were in wheelchairs, and the camp counselors were 14-year-olds who were also handicapped. They all lived in a dilapidated dormitory building that looked like a shack.

The children wouldn't even look at me when I ate lunch with them, and it became obvious that they were suspicious of me and wanted nothing to do with a new director. Dorothy Stults, the physical therapist, was the only supportive person I met. She sat next to me at lunch and reassured me. "Don't let them frighten you. They'll be all right if you'll come."

When I returned to Chicago and told Lucy Carner that I was not interested in the job and didn't feel equipped to han-

31

dle the situation, she would not accept no for an answer. "Don't tell me that," she said. "I understand you've been working with Dr. Dreikurs and have learned how to handle problem situations. You've also had a lot of experience at Hull-House. I can't really say that it is your responsibility to take this job, but if we close the camp, all these children will go back to a miserable summer with parents who would prefer not to have them at home. If you have it in your heart to refuse, go ahead."

Of course I could not hold out after that appeal, so I went to the camp and became their director.

Worse Than I Imagined

It was horrible – more so than I had even imagined. The first night a maintenance man with a wooden leg kept circling my cabin and I could hear this thump . . . thump . . . thump all night long. It scared the living daylights out of me! Dorothy Stults helped me by moving her cot into my cabin in the morning so that I wouldn't be alone.

The next day the same maintenance man shut the water off during my shower. I had just gotten myself covered with soap. Then that afternoon the children refused to mop the floor. Since so many of the campers were spastic, the floor had to be mopped after every meal. First they said they couldn't because there was no water, then they complained about the equipment. When I finally asserted myself enough to suggest that they get buckets of water out of the lake, they then refused to do anything.

Consultation with Rudolf

At this point I telephoned Rudolf and asked for help. He told me exactly what to do and what to say in order to win them over. Each day I called him for advice if I had a problem.

The last straw was when six boys who were not ambulatory got caught in a storm while out on the lake in a boat. The previous director had allowed them to do this kind of thing as one of the privileges she had dispensed, and I had gone along with most of them in order to keep peace with the children. The boys had not returned. I was petrified that these boys had drowned. Dorothy drove me around the lake and we finally found the six of them drinking beer in a tavern.

Rudolf to the Rescue

This time when I called Rudolf I begged him to come out and help me, and he came immediately. We discussed the situation and worked out a solution. That evening I had all the campers convene for a meeting, and this is what I told them.

"I understand how much you loved Margaret, who was your camp director, but I'm not responsible for her not being here. I don't want to be here any more than you want me here, but I have a job to do. Those of you who are unhappy and wish to leave may take a train in the morning. We will make all the transportation arrangements. I'll be happy to have anyone stay who wishes to, but we will have to come to a new agreement about rules. There will be no more privileges until we see if we can get this camp running smoothly."

Eventually the situation worked out well and not one of the campers chose to leave. This is one example of how I began to depend on Rudolf more and more for guidance in new situations. Giving choices and responsibility and requesting help were a few of the Dreikurs techniques which I began using with his coaching. Shifting attention from me to the task to be accomplished had won them over.

Marriage to Rudolf

One day Rudolf said to me, "Now look–what are we doing fooling around like this with telephone calls? Why don't we get married and I can advise you all the time?"

Attracted but Hesitant

By this time I knew I was very attracted to him. It was much later when I realized that most of my attraction to him was based on his similarity to both Leon and Jane Addams. He was courageous and firm when he had to be, like Miss Addams. He didn't worry about failure, but forged straight ahead. Like Leon, he treated me gently and with much tenderness, but still allowed me to be a person in my own right.

However, I was very much afraid of getting married again, and I frankly told him, "Rudolf, you don't know what you're asking for. I really don't want to get married again. How can you possibly live up to this saintly husband I've just lost? I'll constantly be comparing you to him and you'll fall short."

Rudolf Convinces Me

He said, "That's my problem, not yours. I'm willing to take a chance that I'll know how to handle it." So I gave in. We were married in September, 1943.

I still wore the very narrow wedding band that Leon had given me, which was almost worn to a frazzle. Rudolf wanted to marry me in his mother's engagement ring, but I asked him if he'd mind if I continued to wear the original band. He said, "Not only do I not mind, but I'll marry you in that band." He merely added his initials and the date of our marriage to Leon's initials and the date of my first marriage. His kindness and wonderful consideration captivated me. When I came home to his house for the first time, I found Leon's photograph on our dresser. I asked, "What is that doing here?"

He replied, "He was my friend as well as yours. I know that you're going to open the drawer and look at the picture all the time. Why don't we just put it up? When you're ready not to look at it, you'll put it away again." This was the beginning of our marriage.

Becoming a Mother

After we decided to get married, I talked to Rudolf about Eva. "She has been the main woman in your household, the apple of your eye, and I'm somewhat concerned about how she'll respond to me. I've never had a child of my own and want one very much, but a 14-year-old isn't quite a child. It's a difficult age. I wonder what she'll call me."

"That's not our problem," said Rudolf. "Let Eva decide what she wants to call you. You're not going to tell her anything. She'll make up her own mind, and whatever she decides will be fine."

My mother had insisted that we have a formal wedding with a sitdown meal afterward, but there wasn't enough room for everyone to be seated at once. Eva was at the first table and had finished eating before I was seated. When I walked through the room I asked her if she'd had enough to eat. "Yes, Mother," she answered. That was it. She had decided.

Eva Proud to Have Me

Shortly thereafter we went to the theater. She was standing next to me in the washroom and she yelled, "MOTHER, MOTHER!" She wanted everyone to know that she had a mother. She developed a terrific crush on me and a terrible antagonism to her father. She was angry with him for bringing me into the home.

There were several problems that had to be worked out, aside from Eva's displaced anger. She lost all her baggage when she came home from camp soon after we were married, and her room was always a shambles — messy as all getout. Of course, Rudolf helped me with these problems, and we succeeded. I couldn't have done it on my own.

Eva Displayed the Dreikurs' Skill

In spite of the difficulties, Eva did much more to cement our relationship than I. I was more of a pampered wife than she was a spoiled child. She really helped me a great deal.

I was going through a drawer of old linens one day and found some beautiful, large napkins with the letter "S" on them.

35

Eva's mother's name was Stephanie. I said, "Eva, take these and keep them. They belonged to your mother."

She said, "I have only one mother, and her initial is "S," so don't give them to me. They're yours." This was a brief incident, but it was typical of the way in which Eva helped me to feel accepted as her mother.

Thanks to Josy

The other person who was a marvelous help to me was Josy Pollock. Although Rudolf's sister, Bertha, had lived with Eva and her father after they came to this country, it was Josy who had in effect been Eva's mother. She had brought Eva and Eric from Vienna to America. After Josy had made the difficult trip to America with Rudolf's children, she lived nearby and remained very close to the family. Not once did she intrude on Rudolf's relationship with his sister or with me. She came to help me the very first day. She got on her hands and knees and scrubbed the floor. When I admonished her, she said, "We can't afford a maid, and I don't mind doing it, so I'm going to."

It was Josy who taught me how to cook. I had never had to cook for Leon since we ate in the dining room at Hull-House, and I was scared to death to cook for this family. I didn't know how. Josy taught me, and she continued to give Eva her love, attention, and assurance that she was still her "Muttie." There was no animosity or resentment of me, and to this day we have never had any conflict.

Eric Returns

It was after we were married before I met Eric again. His tour of duty in the army was over, and he came to live at our house for a couple of months before going to the university to work on his Ph.D. in psychology. He had served in Europe as a psychologist for the army because a forceps delivery had left Eric with a withered arm which prevented him from being in active service.

Strangely enough, Eric developed the same kind of crush on me that Eva had. In fact, I used to describe him as the tail of my dog—wherever I went, He was right behind me with questions. We did a lot of talking and had the same great relationship that I had with my daughter. Still, I learned the lesson that one could be a "mother" and friend at the same time.

Eric Weds

About this time, Dr. Dreikurs hired an assistant for the first time. His name was Arthur Zweibol. He and his wife Sylvia were separated, and she came to Chicago to finalize the divorce. She was a grammar school teacher, and, while visiting us, met Eric, who was also in the house at the time. He fell in love with her, Sylvia got her divorce and married Eric, and they lived in Urbana for a number of years before their marriage also broke up. He and I have had a very good understanding through the years. He started calling me "Maw" in the beginning, and continued, occasionally, to refer to me in this way until his death in 1984. However, I was always Teetaw to him and we were friends rather than parent and child.

The Lean Years

Over or Underqualified

I did not have a job early in our marriage, and I had trouble finding one. I was considered overly trained and too experienced for a job as a caseworker, but I did not have a college degree, and that was a requirement for an executive position as a supervisor. Social agencies had become very strict about employee qualifications.

Charlotte Carr had many connections and tried to get me a job in a bank, but I had the same problem again. I was not allowed to do clerical work and couldn't be hired as a vice-president. We were becoming a paper world.

Financial Difficulties

Since the war was still going on, and there were working mothers with children who needed care, I finally got a job with the Board of Education, planning programs for after school care. Once again I tried to introduce the Adlerian method but met with resistance from teachers, volunteers and the principal. I stuck with the program, but it lasted less than a year. As I recall, the war ended about then and there was no further financial support for either the program or me.

For two consecutive summers I was the director of a day camp at Jewish People's Institute, but this was just a temporary job.

Rudolf's practice was still quite limited, and if a client cancelled an appointment or didn't show up, we'd lose the $15 he was then charging. Fortunately we didn't have to put Eric through school since he was attending the university on the GI Bill of Rights, and Eva was still in high school. However, it was a difficult time for us. Again, I learned to live with adversity.

Rudolf Accepted All Invitations

Rudolf accepted all invitations to give lectures and went anywhere for any fee. Small women's organizations or PTA groups would hear about him and offer $15, $10, or even $5, and he would gladly go. I'd meet him at the office with a sandwich which he'd eat on the way. I'd go with him and we used whatever surface transportation was available until we had a car.

Sometimes we'd get into very amusing situations. The anxious chairperson of the event would meet us at the door, beaming, and greet us with, "Dr. Dreikurs, it's so wonderful to have you with us," and the first thing Rudolf would say was, "What am I supposed to talk about?"

He never looked at any materials they sent to help him prepare his talks, and of course they were always dismayed at this question immediately before the program was to begin. When he realized they were upset, he'd say, "Don't worry dear. I say the same thing anyway, no matter what you're asking me to talk about. It will be all right." And it was.

One time Rudolf gave a series of five lectures on marriage to the Jewish People's Institute. In the first lecture he debunked the idea that love is more important in marriage than respect and friendship. At the end of the session a little old woman came up to me and asked, "Is he your husband?" "Yes," I answered. "Do I feel sorry for you!" she said. He was often misunderstood in his enthusiasm for and insistence on respect in all relationships.

We continued to have a difficult time financially, although Rudolf had been appointed Professor of Psychiatry in 1942 at the Chicago Medical School. He had to spend a number of hours there but received no remuneration for his work. In spite of these difficulties we pulled through. This taught me the importance of optimism.

Brazil

When the Nazis moved in and Rudolf left Vienna, he first went to Rio. In 1946 Rudolf decided it was time to go back to Brazil. He had started an Adlerian group there in 1937 and had just received a letter from Professor Silva DaMello asking him to return to reactivate this group. Silva assured Rudolf that there would be a university job for him as well as some work at a hospital.

Rudolf's Confidence

Since we would have to pay for our own transportation I felt we couldn't afford to go, but Rudolf said, "Don't worry, we'll find the money." He was in debt from his unsuccessful attempts to rescue his parents from the situation in Europe, so he took a loan on his insurance. "I'll make enough money to pay for transportation, pay off my debts, and pay off my insurance loan," he informed me. I didn't believe him at all. I didn't see how it was possible.

It was summer, and Eva had just finished high school, so we took her with us and she returned in the fall for college. Rudolf assured me that it would be lovely and warm, but I was sure we'd freeze to death because it would be winter there. My expectations were fulfilled when we arrived. It was raining and cold. It was just terrible.

Rudolf did make quite an impression in Brazil, he did make all the money he'd said he would, and we ended up having a marvelous time as well as having a fantastic professional experience. We lived in Rio across the Bay, in a lovely resort, and explored by taking buses through remote fishing villages.

One day while exploring we came upon a stone house being built on a cliff with a breathtaking view of the Bay. Rudolf said, "Let's find the realtor and see if we can buy this house."

I reminded him that we were in debt, didn't have any money to buy a house, and pointed out to him that we wouldn't be able to use it. "You'll see," he said. "I'll have enough money, and if we have a house here we'll come back."

40

We never did buy the house, of course. I had no desire to live in Rio, and although Rudolf wanted to live there, he also wanted to live in Oregon, Jamaica, and many other places. For some reason we always came back to Chicago, and I never really wanted to live anywhere else. Still, I was impressed by his willingness to take risks.

Mourning for Leon

For me, the most significant event during our time in Rio was a conversation I had with Rudolf which, finally, after three years of marriage to him, put an end to my mourning for Leon. We were walking along the beach as the sun was setting, looking across the Bay at the Christ figure and the Sugerloaf Mountains. It was beautiful beyond words, and I started to cry. "Why are you crying?" asked Rudolf. "I'm crying because Leon will never be able to see this and paint it," I answered.

"I'm going to tell you something," he said. "You're not crying for Leon. You're crying for yourself. You're sorry your life has changed. I can accept that and you can continue to be unhappy, but please remember, you only have this moment with me right now. We don't know if we'll have another moment tomorrow, and you can't bring Leon here. Make up your mind."

That was quite a jolt. It was simply said, but the message was very potent, and I stopped mourning at that instant. I no longer needed to hanker for my relationship with Leon. It was finished, and my attitude changed toward Rudolf and our marriage. Directness had brought me into the present. I saw that marriage is a relationship and not just a feeling.

A Partnership

International Travel

Our trip to Brazil in 1946 was the beginning of my international travels with Rudolf. I had no other jobs after the war ended, and from that time on I worked and traveled with him. We began giving workshops in Europe in the early '50s and by 1960 had included Munich, Switzerland, Greece and Israel on our tour. I now follow much the same path each year teaching art therapy, and I have become a traveling ambassador for Individual Psychology.

Writing

At home I helped him with his writing. I had already become a fairly competent Individual Psychologist before we were married. I had by then been studying with Rudolf for almost three years, having had his supervision wherever I worked, and later taking the role of his social worker at the Child Guidance Centers. It was an onging practicum in the theory and methods of Individual Psychology, with continuous feedback from Rudolf. Therefore I could do no more than just help with the mechanical aspects of his writing.

I typed every paper and book as he dictated, but I'd stop him frequently and ask for clarification, more explanation or elaboration on a point, or suggest that he change a section. I might say, "Are you not putting something in here that can be misinterpreted?"

After our first draft was completed, I consulted with an editor. This person was a friend who read the material, sometimes tightened it, and corrected grammatical errors. My grammar was very poor, and, in addition, to our detriment, I had begun to absorb Rudolf's Germanic sentence construction.

My Role

When we traveled I was Rudolf's right hand person. Since I was the only one who knew what he was trying to do or say, in lectures and workshops, he depended on me for feedback as a trained observer. I didn't do this as much in Chicago because he was surrounded by knowledgeable colleagues, but when we were alone on tour he gave me the unique role of sensing the group's reaction to him so that I could signal to him what he should do.

As soon as we appeared in any group he would introduce me and say, "Tee is here not only as my wife, but to fulfill a specific function." Later he would explain, "When I'm in the process of lecturing or demonstrating I can't observe what I'm doing. Tee observes and signals to me so that I know the group's reaction and what needs to be done."

The typical way I did this was by asking questions the people did not dare ask. I became part of the group and sensed their reaction to what Rudolf was doing. I'd win their confidence and give him feedback at the same time by saying out loud whatever they were thinking, sometimes coming to the rescue of whoever was on the hot seat at the time.

For example, Rudolf started one lecture by stating, "In my opinion, the most important element in a parent child relationship is respect." I was immediately aware of the group's resistance to this idea. We were speaking to a new group in Israel, where parents tend to be very protective of their children, wanting them to have all that they had been denied during their childhood. As a result the children are often quite pampered. I could hear the mothers in this group, who were used to smothering their children with love and chicken soup, just buzzing with questions. "What, no love? Respect? Doesn't he think you should love your child?" I raised my hand and asked, "Dr. Dreikurs, are you saying that love is not important, or that parents shouldn't love their children?" Rudolf then corrected their impressions and they listened when he went on to explain the difference between the kind of love which shows respect and that which is possessive in the typical authoritarian family. He won the audience over. The mothers began to see the differences between democratic and autocratic love.

The Gift of Courage

It was due to Rudolf's genius — or, as he would say, his "nose for things" — that he realized I could step into this role in spite of my being a timid, inward kind of person. This was one of his greatest gifts to me. Through him I became a courageous person who could be a leader, reach out to others and win the confidence of a group in a very short time. He helped me overcome my feeling of being just an appendage, and in this way really prepared me for my subsequent independent, international role as an art therapist.

Surprisingly enough, I didn't even realize what Rudolf had done for me until a few years ago when Achi Yotam, from Israel, said to me, "It's amazing how courageous you are and how much you can encourage others." It was Rudolf who had turned me into a courageous person by giving me the opportunity to speak up in my role as devil's advocate.

Not too infrequently Rudolf and I would end up having a public altercation when I took exception to something he'd said, in an attempt to let him know what the audience was thinking. As a rule this was a delightful experience for the group, and they were reassured that a couple can have differences and still love each other. Occasionally he would forget my role and take me seriously, especially if my manner in asking questions was too provocative. Then he'd say, "Tee, you should know better than that. You know what I mean!"

Even Rudolf's manner was encouraging to me. He was inclined to be very outspoken. He didn't mince words when he was critical of a therapist, and spoke to his own clients in a forceful way. Although he gave me the feeling that I was special, he didn't coddle me as I believe Leon did, and this helped me to develop my own courage. When he saw me going in a faulty direction he would be very direct and sharp about it. Although I am not sharp with my art therapy students, I have learned to be direct.

Expressing My Creativity

It was Rudolf who called my attention to the fact that I essentially react to situations on an intuitive, spontaneous level. I doubt my intellectual capacity to work out anything academically. Hence, when Rudolf first began introducing me as his best trained student, I froze up completely. He stopped doing that and let me sit back, listen, and observe. Then I could relax, and use my training and creative skills to respond freely to all the input I got from the group and what Rudolf was doing. As long as I didn't feel responsible for living up to someone's expectations, and it wasn't an academic assignment, I was able to help out with questions and ideas which others had perhaps not thought about. Ideas seem to come as naturally to me as the flowing waves when I'm not hung up on the idea that "I must perform, I must be brilliant."

Stories Help

I also use stories to get me off the hook when I don't know how to answer an academic question, and I'm reminded of one now concerning this very tactic. It's a story of two gentlemen who sat on a park bench in New York, discussing many things. After they had exhausted all possible topics, one said to the other, "You know what, my friend? Life is like a glass of tea." The other looked at him in astonishment and said, "Why is life like a glass of tea?" The first responded, "Don't ask me! I'm not a philosopher."

This story fits me to a Tee(!). I can work spontaneously but I can't explain what I'm doing theoretically. I utilize all that I've learned from Blanche, Jane Addams, Leon and Rudolf, as well as what I've absorbed from my experience in art, social work, group work and Individual Psychology. However, I often can't identify specifically how I learned a particular method or where I got an idea. I'm a doer, not a thinker, although a lot of thinking must take place without my conscious awareness.

In all my years of traveling with Rudolf I gradually acquired the same feeling he had, of truly being a member of the world community. This was largely due to the manner in which he treated me wherever we went. Because we returned frequently to the same places, people accepted us as their friends and we were able to be a part of their lives. It was a precious and rare experience.

These contacts made it possible for me to become known as a personality in my own right, and paved the way for me to come back in later years to give workshops in art therapy.

The Fifth Life Task

Because of our travels, I feel very much a part of many societies. This is especially true in Israel, and I'm sure this is due to my Jewish heritage.

Is There a God?

I believe both Leon and Rudolf were more or less agnostic. They had faith that man belonged to something, but couldn't identify it. They resisted the idea that something outside mankind had control, and they were convinced that man has always made his own problems.

Rudolf used to say, "I neither believe nor deny. If you can give me proof that there's a God or a supernatural being, I'll gladly acknowledge it. However, I have an assignment here on earth. I work with my fellow men and women, and I am not speculating on control from outside."

I accepted this attitude and began to think the same way, but I have never in my own mind denied the concept of God. It's an important word, and all human beings have their own idea about God. In Judaism God is amorphous. There is no relationship to a human image. He comes as a shining light. For me God is the unknowable. Someday I may know, but I don't right now.

I am not aware that my religious heritage affects my work at all, except in the content of the stories I tell. In fact, when a young woman approached me during an art therapy workshop in Vancouver recently, and spoke Hebrew to me, I was amazed at my own response. I immediately felt a close bond with her; therefore, I must not be completely free of the sense of embeddedness in this group.

Identification with the Israelis

Rudolf said he could identify more with being an Israeli than with being a Jew, because the Israelis were building a new nation based on principles of equality, and were confronting their problems daily. He identified much more with these people than with David and Goliath.

I have had the sensation of being caught up in antiquity when I'm in Israel. The present seems only a part of an ongoing evolution. The first time I experienced this, I'm quite sure I had a brief psychotic episode. Rudolf refused to believe it since he had the very same sensation at the same time.

We were standing on the roof of a minaret on Mt. Zion, at the place where King David was born. Jews did not have access to this place in the old days, but tourists now came in droves, with guides of different religious persuasions who talked about the city of Jerusalem. As I looked at this ancient city with the lights shimmering below, and listened to the guide talk about what went on ages ago, I experienced an intense déjà vu sensation. I *must* have been here before.

I roused myself and turned to Rudolf. "I think I'm having a psychotic episode. I'm sure I've been here before." He said, "That's not psychotic!" He was experiencing it too. Perhaps it was not psychotic but mystic.

The Adlerian Art Therapist

It was in 1962, I believe, that Dr. Bernard Shulman came to our house for lunch one day to discuss with Rudolf an idea about offering a different type of therapeutic experience to his psychiatric patients at St. Joseph Hospital. This idea was the beginning of my career as an art therapist. Up until this point I had been an adjunct to Rudolf in his work and, with one exception, had not even painted after Leon's death.

Brief Art Interlude

This one exception was a two or three week period in 1958 when we were in Jamaica. It was beautiful, there was a wonderful studio, and Rudolf persuaded me to do a few paintings of the black people whom I adored.* I used pastels and charcoal only, and it was fun, although I was conscious of the fact that I was doing it to please Rudolf. I couldn't have cared less whether I did it or not. I treated these portraits as an enjoyable exercise and did a whole batch of them, some in only 15 minutes. I didn't think much of them at the time and discarded or gave away most of them, but Rudolf rescued two and had them framed.

I now enjoy these very much. They are very strong, and much different from my work years before. I knew that if I ever started to paint again I could never recapture my previous style. I'd start with something completely new.

Rudolf was very frustrated with me because I stopped painting. It was his idea that I owed the world my great talent. Well, I never thought I had a great talent and my response was, "I don't feel the need for it. My painting days were a combination of my life with Blanche as a little girl and with Leon in my first marriage. Now my life is with you and what you're doing, it's still creative, and I feel fulfilled." I did not

---

*Tee has always had a preference for painting black people, which may or may not be related to her identification with them since her childhood when she was referred to as "the dark one" or "schwartzeh."

need paint. In my mind, painting was still one thing, psychology another.

Work at St. Joseph

Shulman, who was Rudolf's first assistant and associate in private practice, had just been given a psychiatric unit at St. Joseph's and wanted Rudolf to help him train the staff in Adlerian theory and methods. He envisioned the unit being organized on a milieux therapy basis, which would provide a different experience for patients.

While I was serving lunch, both Rudolf and Bernie looked at me and said, "Why don't you come and help us? With your experience in group dynamics and group painting, social work, and your knowledge of Individual Psychology, you could develop an art therapy program for us. Just experiment. We have no rules or prescriptions for you. It's all yours." This approach from the very beginning freed me from the pressure of having to produce something which required immediate approval. I could be as innovative as I wished, and in fact did try many things with patients as I worked out my program.

In the beginning I worked only with Bernie's patients, although other psychiatrists also had patients in this unit. Fortunately there were no objections to my doing this. We used the library, which was a rather small room, and an announcement was made each time on the loudspeaker. "Would all of Dr. Shulman's patients please proceed to the library." No explanation was given. The program I developed is explained more fully in the following section of this book.

Travel After Rudolf's Death

I worked at the hospital periodically, a few months at a time, because of the traveling I did with Rudolf. It wasn't until after his death in 1972 that I began working on a regular basis. I also continued to travel as we had done before, giving art therapy sessions in foreign countries as well as the United States. My first invitation was from the Washington, D.C., area. Then I was asked to visit Vancouver, B.C. I worked with lay groups and professionals who wanted to learn my methods.

In the winter of 1973, I arranged a tour which started in Switzerland. From there I went on to Germany, Greece and Israel, taking the same path that Rudolf had blazed. I have since broadened the number of places I visit, but I've returned each year, so that now there are well organized groups of people in these countries who work with me in planning my sessions and carrying forth my work.

Work at the Institute

A few years after Rudolf died I began teaching at the Alfred Adler Institute of Chicago. In the beginning I had weekend sessions about three times a year. Art Therapy was later incorporated into the curriculum, and when the graduate school was established, it became an elective, called "The Use of Art in Counseling," in the master's degree program.

I began serving on the Board of the Institute shortly after Rudolf died, although I wanted to resign and not have anything to do with it. It was Bernie Shulman who persuaded me to stay with them. He said to me, "We need your ideas, and we need you to be our conscience." I've never really understood what he meant by that. Up until Rudolf's death I felt that I was active in the Institute only by marriage. I was Rudolf's co-counselor with families, and again played the role of asking the right questions for a group, or summing up the session.

The administration did turn to me at times for advice, and I served on the planning board from its inception in the early '50s. I occasionally worked with clients if the regular counselor didn't show up at the Institute, but otherwise I've never done any counseling on my own. But it did not feel like a "conscience," and I certainly did not feel adequate as an independent counselor.

Minus to Plus

I remember one horrendous incident when Bob Powers asked me to take over a session with a family while he was out of town. He'd gotten the date mixed up, so the family hadn't been informed in advance, he had changed Rudolf's usual format so that it was not a comfortable routine for me, and Bob had become very popular with this family, with whom he'd been working for quite some time. When I appeared on the scene the mother didn't want to talk to me and I didn't know what to do. It was a disaster.

I said to her, "You and I have a common problem. What is it?" She couldn't guess, and neither could the audience, made up of other parents and students, which is the typical way family counseling is done in the Adlerian Family Education Centers. I answered for them, "You don't want me to counsel you, and I don't want to be here. What are we going to do about this situation?"

We went on with the interview and I thought the whole thing was a complete flop, but when we finished, the group members said that it had been a highly charged example of how to turn an impossible situation into a learning experience. As Rudolf used to say to me, "You always remember the one bad time and forget the other nine wonderful ones." The bad times can become good times—if we work on them.

Center Stage

I was shocked to realize recently that I now actually enjoyed being on center stage when I present art therapy workshops to people all over the world. I love the role. I adore it. However, I think it reflects a slight touch of vanity, because I continue to rely heavily on Rudolf. I'm constantly thinking, "If Dreikurs were here, what would he do?"

Dreikurs' Contribution

Rudolf's greatest contribution to me in my work was the simplistic brilliance of his interviewing techniques and his formulation of the hidden reasons* through guessing.** These techniques have been a great strength to me. I understood what he was doing and later discovered that I had become adept with these also.

---

*The "hidden reason" refers to that aspect of the individual's private logic (idiosyncratic perceiving and thinking) which rationalizes behavior so as to make it acceptable to oneself. The hidden reason is largely unknown to the individual. The therapist can make guesses to determine the hidden reason. These guesses are in keeping with the knowledge of the client's movement which is already clear to the therapist. For example, the therapist might say: "Do you know why you did that (stating what the individual behavior actually was)?" The client usually responds with "I don't know." The therapist then may say, "What were you thinking just at the time when you took that action?", "What did you tell yourself?" or "Could it be you said to yourself, 'If that's the way he is going to act I may as well do whatever I please'?" An example in art therapy might be the patient who refuses to paint. Here the hidden reason might be "Unless I can be as good as Rembrandt, I won't even try."

In art therapy, as in other forms of group therapy, the therapist can ask the group for help in uncovering the client's hidden reason. The therapist

Rudolf followed a very logical sequence when he interviewed a client. He avoided any irrelevant material, and immediately responded to whatever comment lent itself to further exploration. He didn't bother to keep gathering facts ("factophilia") but began to work immediately with the information he had at hand.

When I am working with a group teaching art therapy or actually doing it with hospital patients, I find myself even using some of Rudolf's phrases, such as "Keep in mind" or "It is amazing how . . . " Much of Rudolf has become a part of me, so that when I am successful in my work and feel encouraged about what I am able to do, there is still an awareness of my underlying reliance on him.

The Influence of Blanche

Although my work is influenced greatly by Rudolf, Blanche had probably the strongest influence on my life. Because of her I began painting, went to Hull House, met Jane Addams and Leon Garland, and even Rudolf, to whom I went for help when I was working with the delinquents at Hull-House. My life and my work became one. And, perhaps, I am now becoming one too.

Growing Confidence

I have developed much more self-confidence over the years, largely due to the encouragement of others, but I still can't really believe that I have a skill of my own. I never thought of myself as an artist: Leon was the artist. And I resent anyone

---

says to the group, "Put yourself in her place. If you had done that, what would you be saying to yourself in order to justify your behavior?" Several group members offer guesses. When the correct guess is hit upon, the client will give a reflexive recognition such as "That's it." Or the client will smile, even laugh. If after a number of guesses without a positive response from the client, the therapist asks the client, "Which one of those ideas came closest?" Based upon the client statement as to which came closest, the therapist or group members can make further guesses.

**The guessing method which was developed by Adler (Adler, 1969) and redefined by Dreikurs (Dreikurs, 1977) relies on the stochastic method: divining the truth through conjecture. Based upon previous knowledge of the client's movement and prior guesses, the therapist comes closer and closer to a complete understanding of the client's pattern of movement. Guessing saves much time in understanding the client and making this knowledge available to the client.

who says that Rudolf would never have gotten as far as he did without me. I don't think it's a matter of my feeling secondary to the other person. I felt part of Leon and later Rudolf. I needed them and their strength. perhaps it was because I am essentially not a very brave person. I don't venture forth on my own. My pattern has always been to follow, to rely on my allies to set the course for me, and then I gladly follow along. I don't think of myself as a leader.

I'm sure this pattern developed when I was a small child. I remember goading my little brother into fighting my big sister because she was bugging me, and I continued over the years to assume that I needed someone else to fight my battles for me. I never believed that I did anything for my own satisfaction. It was always for someone else. I painted for Leon, I co-counseled for Rudolf, and I never felt I was very good at anything on my own.

Now that I find myself enjoying the role of teaching art therapy all over the world, I realize that my persistent feelings of inadequacy are fictions that I maintained to avoid the responsibility that goes with leadership. Now that I am out there being a leader I have mixed emotions about it. I both enjoy it and also feel that I must not really deserve this recognition and satisfaction. Actually I am greatly encouraged that at my age I am not dying on top first!

Bringing Therapy and Art Together

Art therapy fulfills me, because it encompasses all of my life's training and experiences. I am putting together all that I have gleaned from life and using all my skills. Art therapy is stimulating and an ongoing creative expression for me, so that I am energized and feel encouraged to continue after each session.

There are many people who have influenced me throughout my life, and at this point I realize that nothing has been lost to me. I am synthesizing what I've learned and am experiencing much satisfaction from this creative endeavor while at the same time feeling grateful for the wonderful relationships I've had with Blanche, Jane Addams, Leon, and Rudolf.

Part II

Art Therapy

Is Art Therapy
Really Psychotherapy?

Art therapy for me implies help through art. This medium can help people feel better about themselves, change their perception of themselves, or merely provide an enjoyable experience. It can encourage those participants who are depressed to pursue other possibilities for enjoyment. After participating in the art activities they often have a sense of well-being, even of elation, from the feeling of accomplishment and contribution. Art therapy can help people function in any area of their lives or it can be a softening up process through which they become more aware of their movement in life and can choose, if they wish, to make lifestyle changes through psychotherapy.*

Lifestyle Changes

In psychotherapy the therapist works with clients to assess the lifestyle, the life pattern, to evaluate the faulty conclusions

---

*Whether art therapy is psychotherapy or not may be best answered through the definitions of "guidance," "counseling," and "therapy." "Guidance" implies giving advice or education directly to the client. "Counseling" is providing education in a strategic manner so as to improve the possibility of the client accepting and using the education. This education is designed to help the client to better cope with the life tasks. "Therapy" refers to offering education in the form of guidance or counseling, but this approach additionally results in changes in the client's lifestyle. These changes do not usually involve a new fictive goal or methods of operation (how one moves toward the goal), but they do result in greater breadth to the lifestyle. Adler referred to this greater breadth as "elasticity" (Adler, 1956). These changes result from the confrontation of the client with his or her lifestyle and understanding ways in which the lifestyle can be used more flexibly and more effectively.

Art therapy is a most rapid method in assisting people to confront their lifestyle. In the hands of a skilled therapist, the confrontation is encouragingly presented so that the clients can see new possibilities for using what they have more effectively. Is art therapy really therapy? It is when used by a skilled therapist, which is true with any therapeutic approach.

they have about their place in life, and to help them change their ineffective patterns of behavior. The therapist may guide the clients in order to broaden the lifestyle to allow for more freedom of movement within the established pattern without changing the basic mistakes.

In an art therapy session participants may discover, contrary to their previous belief, that they can use their hands to produce something very satisfying. This may be a revelation which gives them a different self-concept, more self-acceptance, but it doesn't necessarily change the lifestyle.

Nevertheless, I have seen basic apperceptions* change in art therapy. It is not my goal to change the lifestyle or one's basic mistakes. It is my intention, however, to enable participants to see themselves and how they function more clearly so that they are able to choose alternatives. Art therapy seems to be such a powerful technique that one is immediately confronted with one's lifestyle almost from the beginning of the task in the most unexpected way. In addition, the experience of going through a session and ending with "Wow, did I do this?" is therapy in a sense because it immediately gives people a different view of their ability, and some possibilities that might be available to them.

Realization of Life's Emptiness

The most frequent response I get from participants is the recognition that something is missing in their lives that they had not previously realized. For some reason, when participants go through the different painting exercises, this feeling surfaces and is expressed during the discussion period.

I'm not sure why it's the experience of painting which elicits the recognition of this void. Is it the tactile pleasure, the sensual feeling enhanced by the use of paints on paper, or a spiritual experience? Is it being creative in the company of others, or a sense of being in partnership with my creator: I also can create?

---

*Apperception is the way in which people view themselves and the external world. It includes the current situation, their views, their pattern of movement and the goal toward which they are striving. People interpret a percept according to their knowledge and personal biases (Adler, 1929).

General Methods

BEGINNING

Greeting the Group

Quite by accident I stumbled upon a unique way of greeting a new group which allows me to establish a different kind of relationship than the patients or participants have heretofore experienced. I happened one time to be standing at the door when the group members approached, and instead of having them all come in, I greeted them one by one, shook their hands, and said, "I am Tee Dreikurs. I would like it very much if you would call me by my first name. What is your name? Would you permit me to use your first name or do you prefer that I use your last name?"

I have since changed this greeting slightly, based on an experience I had when I was hospitalized. All of the young nurses came in and called me Sadie and I resented it. I came to the conclusion that there are some people who probably don't want to be called by their first names and may not want to call me Tee. Therefore, I now say, "I'd like it very much if you would call me by my first name, but if you have any objection, please call me Mrs. Dreikurs. Do you want me to call you by your first or last name?"

The manner in which the person approaches me or pulls away, the clammy hand or the firm grip, whether eyes meet mine or are averted, and what is said offer me an opportunity to use a mild form of "antisuggestion," a creation of Dreikurs, which Viktor Frankl subsequently termed "paradoxical intention" (Dreikurs, 1967), to encourage participants who are fearful or resistant. For example, with the hospital patient who says, "I'm too sleepy. I really don't know why I'm here. I thought we were going to get medication," I might respond, "If you're too sleepy, go back to your room and sleep. When you feel you're awake enough and want to return, please come back." Invariably the response is, "I'm not *that* sleepy. I think I'll come in."

Whenever I encounter a negative attitude I make a point of responding in a way which clarifies the reason for not wanting to participate and is accepting at the same time. I try to swing with the participant's mood without denying objections or hesitations. If someone says, "I can't draw a straight line," I might respond with, "Go ahead and draw a crooked one."

In my summation and rationale for greeting people at the door, I explain that this gesture helps me to work better. The act of coming toward them rather than waiting in the room lessens my authoritarian image and helps to establish an egalitarian relationship. Giving myself to them in this way takes away the feeling of my being a teacher or the expert, or of more importance than they.

Obtaining Permission of the Group

I have discovered that it is very important, especially with a patient population, to get the permission of the group before proceeding with any activity. If my goals and the goals of the group are in line, we can work together; otherwise we are at cross purposes.

For instance, I might say at the beginning of an inservice group with professionals, "I am following Dreikurs' model of demonstrating first and discussing theory later." Some sophisticated psychologists may object to this approach. If I am working with patients or lay people I often begin with, "Are you willing to experiment with me? Are you willing to go along with me and later talk about what we did and why?"

Winning Cooperation

When there is someone who objects or who is rebellious, as is often the case with teenagers, I do not proceed without winning the person over. If I went ahead anyway, the rebellion might fester and infect the entire group. I usually elicit cooperation at this point by guessing the reason for the objection, thereby letting participants know that I understand them.

With a patient population or with an adolescent group, my guess might be, "Is it possible that you want to show me that you're smarter than I am, that you can't learn anything from me?" Or, "Perhaps you want to do it your way, and no one is going to tell you what to do."

In the case of the sophisticated group of professionals, an example is "I may be all wrong, but it is possible that you think it's going to be a waste of your time to sit here and watch me demonstrate unless you know the theory first? Are you the kind of person who wants to know exactly what, when, and how you're going to do something before you begin?"

If someone is not willing to join in the group activity as it is structured, and for some reason, we are not able to guess the reason, I usually say something like, "Please paint by yourself and the rest of us will play the game. Come and join us when you're ready."

Encouraging Creativity

Since we are all creatures of creation, there must of necessity be something in us that is also creative. This creativity has often been hidden, denied, or suppressed through faulty education. I say to each new group, "It is my purpose to help you realize your creativity." Although this may be encouraging to most participants, some may react negatively. They may be thinking, "Oh, she just doesn't know me." Therefore, I always stop and ask for their reactions. "Tell me what you think about what I just said."

A discussion on creativity follows and I usually have the opportunity to ask group members how they came to the conclusion that they were not creative. We then recreate in discussion the point at which they were discouraged and no longer felt they could be a creative human being. It's important to work on faulty notions and to consider alternatives from the first art therapy session.

ENHANCEMENT OF SOCIAL INTEREST

Sharing Expectations

My central thrust in art therapy is the enhancement of a feeling of belonging, of having a place. I touch on this lightly with the group before beginning the first session, explaining that humans are social beings for whom a sense of belonging is crucial. If we are left alone long enough we would probably lose all the qualities that make us human.

For this reason I then ask each member of the group what their expectations are, what they anticipate getting from this group, and encourage them to tell the group something about themselves. In the case of a patient group, I might ask, "What do you think painting is like? What do you think about painting? Have you ever painted before? When you're not in the hospital how do you spend your time? Do you work? Tell us something about yourself." I make a concerted effort to let them know that I'm interested in them as individuals.

Verbal Feedback

Verbal communication enhances the use of art as a nonverbal method of communication and is a valuable tool for increasing social interest in the group. Not only am I able to more accurately perceive what is going in the minds of participants, but each of them can observe the reactions of others and begin to better understand one another. They also become more involved in the projects as they participate in the process. Therefore, with each new group I explain that I will frequently ask them what I am doing, not as a quiz but so that I'll know what they're thinking and can use their ideas in the activities or discussion.

Eliciting as much verbalization as possible allows me to counteract or diffuse some negative undercurrents. This tends to solidify the group. In addition to the effect on the group, it enhances my own creativity and furthers my own social interest. I accept all responses without judgment.

COUNTERACTING THE FEAR OF FAILURE

Use of Colored Paper

Even before we begin our first project, I ask for reactions of the group to some of my methods — for instance, the use of colored paper and background music. After summarizing their ideas about the colored paper, I add my own reason in the following way. "If you have never painted before and have worries about being able to do anything, just putting one color on another will be pretty to look at and you'll be encouraged to continue. The two colors may give you an idea, whereas the white paper may frighten some people."

Music

As a rule, I use rather quiet, unobstrusive and soothing music during the activity, and I ask participants why they think I do this. When there are no more possible explanations given, I say, "Yes, everything you said is true, but I do it primarily to take your mind away from the immediate situation which may be threatening, and encourage you to concentrate on the music and let it, rather than your thoughts, guide your hand."

It's my experience that the music helps to get people started. I usually suggest that participants listen to the music, let it penetrate their minds and start to paint when there are no more troubling thoughts. However, an occasional patient rebels with an objection such as, "I hate music and I can't stop worrying," at which time I would say, "Don't listen to the music. It's quite all right. You're not obliged to listen." The patient might then say, "I can't help it, the music comes through anyway," to which I'd respond, "Would you like to use some cotton? There's some right here and if you'd like to use it, you'll hear very little of the music."

Later I might concentrate on that patient and deal with the comment about not being able to stop worrying, again intensifying the symptom in order to ultimately diminish it. For example, I'd say, "I don't think you're worrying very much. See if you can put more worry on your paper." This is another form of antisuggestion.

Enjoyment of the Task

In art therapy I want participants to experience something rather unique in our society – enjoyment of the task without regard for approval or success. Hospital patients as well as many others in our society are quite discouraged and are often terribly afraid that they are absolutely worthless and have no chance of ever being useful or successful. Everything I do with any group is oriented toward the reduction of this fear, and most of the activities, because they involve shared rather than individual responsibility, help to release the tension and anxiety associated with the fear of failure. For this reason and to encourage social interest, I have participants prepare the materials for group projects rather than having everything all ready for them.

Permission to Fail

When the participants are a very discouraged group, as with patients, it is essential that they have my permission to fail. "You don't have to do anything you don't feel like doing. You may fight me if you wish. I'm not going to force you to do anything." I don't even use the word try. However, I make every effort to counteract the fear of failure so that they'll be willing to go along with the activities.

My own approach as the art therapist establishes an atmosphere, whether it's one of anxiety, uncertainty, apprehension, need for success, or enjoyment in the activity and group process. Being honest with a group about one's feelings or disabilities promotes a relationship of equality and encourages participants to take the risk of joining group projects.

Without a Personal Stake

As Adler said, you can't have a personal stake in what you're doing ("Ich habe mein Sach' auf nicht gestellt.") I have discovered that the results are far less satisfactory or productive if one equates one's worth with the outcome of a session. If you don't have a personal stake in your work as an art therapist you can be more flexible and can more effectively encourage participants by giving them permission to be imperfect. I remember Dreikurs saying, "Let the chips fall where they may." I approach a group with this attitude in mind and remind myself that "I am here to do a job and I have something to offer which may or may not be of value."

Please keep in mind (a phrase Rudolf often used which I have incorporated into my own vocabulary) that intimate exposure to Dreikurs gave me a great advantage as a beginning art therapist. The fear of making mistakes was always mitigated by the fact that I knew I could go home to Rudolf afterward and he would help me work out any difficulties I had. However, I was surprised the first time to discover that he wouldn't tell me what to do. He asked me questions instead, as I now do with all my groups.

Honesty

Being honest with participants was advantageous in a way I had not anticipated. Since I have a hearing problem and at times am not well enough to join in myself, I am handicapped

64

to a certain extent. I discovered that being honest about this encouraged participants to become more involved in the activities, and as they contributed more, feelings of self-worth and social interest were enhanced.

For example, I might say, "I've had a very bad day and really don't feel well. I need your help. Would you take over and let me be a participant?" Invariably one or two will volunteer to decide on the project for that day and others will volunteer to lead the discussion, etc.

When I first tried talking openly about my hearing problem I was afraid of the group's reaction. I had said, "You see, I have a hearing aid and can't always hear what you're saying. Will you help me? You could talk a little louder or I could come closer to you so that I may hear you better." I decided to ask the participants how they had felt about my saying this. The response was, "We feel good about it. Thank goodness you have something wrong with you too. It makes us feel better." I came to the conclusion that what you do in art therapy is probably not as important as how you do it.*

TECHNICAL CONSIDERATIONS

Charts

I have found it helpful not to read charts when I work with patients in the hospital. I approach the patient population in the same way as I would any group of people. I do not think of them as sick. Dreikurs used to say if you make a negative prognosis based on a diagnosis of a patient, you'll give up and not work with the attitude that anything is possible; or if you make a very positive prognosis you may expect too much of yourself and be shattered if you should fail; therefore, make no diagnosis, no prognosis — wait and see. Similarly, Jane Addams refused to let anyone at Hull House keep case histories, fearing that the record would condition the reader in a certain way, prohibiting an objective perspective on the current situation.

---

*This idea is consistent with Adler's statement that "Individual Psychology is a psychology of use, not of possession" (Ansbacher and Ansbacher, 1956). It's not what you have, but how you use it that counts.

Observation not Permitted

I do not permit anyone to observe art therapy sessions because it inhibits the participants, but visitors are invited to join the group and participate in the projects for the duration of the visit. In a hospital setting patients become guides for the newcomers, who are usually other professionals, assisting them in their adjustment to our ongoing group process. This helps the patients immensely because they have the opportunity to contribute something to others. They also see that the experts in the helping profession are in many ways no different from themselves. Professionals, too, are nervous about painting, hesitant about joining in, fearful of exposing themselves, and have questions about life values.

My Observations

However, for me as the art therapist, observation is of utmost importance. In the beginning I painted with the group but I stopped doing this for two reasons. I discovered that no matter how much I tried not to, I would influence what happened in the group and alter the final product in some way, and I could not observe what was going on as closely when I was working myself.

My observation of participants has to be done in a most unobtrusive manner in order to insure that they are not inhibited, and I rarely take notes. While they think I'm just sitting and waiting for them to complete their projects, I'm really observing each one of them carefully to see how they go about their work and what their body movement tells me. Do they approach the task with confidence or does it occur only in certain situations?

I have noticed that after a group has painted together three or four times, some of the caution dissipates and individuals become part of the project, relying on the others to help out if a mistake is made. The assurance of shared responsibility often changes a person's movement, so it is essential that I observe throughout the entire process.

Sharing Observations with Participants

If participants are professionals, or students in training with me, I discuss my observations of them later (the manner in which they approached the activity, selection of paintings they liked, how they hung them on the wall, spacing, etc.) to emphasize the importance of observation in their own art therapy practice and to point out the significance of all behavior in personality assessment.

I may also discuss some of my observations with groups of participants who are not professionals but who are emotionally stable enough to profit from some of the comments. With an inpatient hospital population, however, I rarely discuss any interpretations unless we have worked together for a long time. If they have conducted some sessions themselves, and have begun to understand more about the process, I may then state some of my observations. In general I don't see the usefulness of encouraging patients to observe the behavior of other group members.

Group Projects

THE CAROUSEL

The first painting project I use with each new group is the carousel. This assignment is most easily done on a long table. I begin after the materials are all prepared, participants have had an opportunity to get to know me and each other, and I have done what I can to encourage cooperation and creativity.

Directions

The explanation of the game goes like this. "Choose one piece of paper, stand in front of it, and listen to the music. When the music is fully penetrating you, start to paint. After a short period of time I will ask you to change, and at that time you will move to the next paper to your right, paint on it, and so on around the table. The papers remain in their original places and you move around the table to each one. When we are done, you will have a chance to paint one of your own."

Advantages of Group Movement

Having participants stand continually during this exercise saves time. However, when working with hospital patients it is beneficial to have them sit while painting, then get up, walk around their chairs, and sit down at the next chair when changing positions. This provides more exercise, helps increase circulation, and seems to be an acceptable compromise for the depressed patient who would prefer not to move at all, and the restless, excited youth or agitated patient for whom moving around is their cup of tea. In addition, when participants get up out of their seats and move to the next place, they are literally walking away from their previous work and starting afresh on something new.

Individuals become more sensitive to their neighbors' reactions because of the group's proximity, and the sharing of this common assignment becomes a unifying experience. The movement around the table is actually like a dance. The group moves together to the music in a rhythmic wavelike pattern around the table. When to say "change" depends on the mood or rhythm of the group. If several appear to be stifled and not know what to paint, or if some are messing up the paintings in front of them, changing more quickly provides an opportunity to have a fresh start, and the new painting often suggests a direction.

Observing the Lifestyle

While the group is engaged in this project, I am constantly observing what's happening. I maintain an overview of all participants, so that I am aware of hesitation, assertiveness, or timidity without deliberately focusing on an individual person. As they move around the table, each one experiences a challenge with each new painting. The way in which this challenge is met reveals the individual's own pattern of movement, or lifestyle.*

When the papers are quite full and each person has had the opportunity to work on a number of paintings, I ask everyone to stop and paint one of their own, after which we all move to another area where we can discuss what happened during the project.

Discussion

A question I always ask at this time is, "Did you prefer working in the group or by yourself?" The answers are extremely informative, and group members become more aware of their own uniquenesses as well as areas of commonality. There are several typical kinds of responses I hear to this question.

Those who prefer to work on their own tend to be strong leaders, loners, or have feelings of inadequacy. Strong leaders often find it difficult to subdue themselves, or their expertise if they are trained painters, in order to cooperate with the group. This project tests their ability to meet the needs of the situation.

The loner usually expresses a preference for working in isolation as protection from others who might interfere with

---

*Dreikurs often described lifestyle as the person's movement in life (Dreikurs, 1960).

preconceived plans or invade valuable privacy. They say something like, "I didn't want anyone to mess up what I started."

Feelings of Inferiority

Others report fear of spoiling someone else's work, either because it was perceived as quite beautiful the way it was, or because of a sense of their own inadequacy in the situation. If the person expresses this fear of spoiling a painting without more explanation, I ask further questions to determine if this feeling of inferiority* exists, so that we can talk about it.

Many participants prefer working with the group, usually because of the experience of shared responsibility for the final project, or the challenging choices each new painting offers as they go around the table. Those who appreciate the group's support feel more comfortable when several people contribute to each painting. I often hear statements like "If I make a mistake, someone else will do something to make it look better," or "If we goof, we all goof together, and if we make a beautiful picture, the whole group feels rewarded for it."

Selecting Three

When we've finished discussing how everyone felt about working in this group project, I ask them to look around at all the paintings. "Please take your time, walk around, look at them all, and decide which three appeal most to you. Leave them where they are and come back and sit down."

I ask one person at a time to hang their three choices on the wall where we can look at them. Then I suggest that the group make comments about what these selections tell us about that individual. "Please respond in a nonjudgmental way so that people do not feel accused. Remember that you are making suggestions which may reflect your own bias. If you phrase your remarks in a tentative manner, the person has a chance to consider some possibilities and agree or disagree without becoming angry or defensive. Actually, you tell us something

---

*Adler refers to "feeling inferior" as a normal response which all people experience in the face of their own desire for perfection. It is only when people demonstrate or act on their feelings of inferiority that they are said to have an "inferiority complex."

70

about yourself when you offer a suggestion so in fact this will be a chance for us all to learn about each other."

When we are finished discussing each set of three paintings, and all interpretations have been considered, there are usually one or two general conclusions which are made by the group in consensus with the individual who made the selections. It is very enlightening then to look at this person's own painting and how it completes the pattern suggested by the three selections.

How each participant approaches the task of hanging these paintings on the wall, and the choices made in their placement, are also illustrative of the individual's movement in life, or lifestyle. Regular balanced spacing suggests orderliness, whereas a haphazard arrangement may indicate a careless attitude or disregard for rules and regulations. A person who tends to be indecisive often takes a lot of time arranging their selections, changing the composition several times.

An Example

I remember one young woman who hung her three selections quite close together. She had chosen a painting with very dark, heavy, completely enclosed circles covering the entire paper. Her second choice had many small black lines on it as on a cardiograph, but also suggestive of nails. The third was a painting of a young girl wearing a pretty hat. The one of circles happened to be her own painting, so that the grouping was complete.

After all the group comments had been shared, I asked her, in my usual fashion, if she'd like me to contribute my ideas as well. She gave her permission and I offered a possible interpretation, speaking in the first person as if I were she. "My life at this time is a series of difficulties and I go around and around without finding a solution. There doesn't seem to be any way out of these painful problems that are surrounding me. If only I could be a happy young girl again."

This young woman began to cry and it was a dramatic moment for the group. She said, "My mother's been wanting me to go into therapy. I've been refusing, but now I'll go. If I express so much about myself in these selections, I know there is something that I have to find out about myself that I don't yet know."

71

Feedback and Evaluation

In this case it wasn't necessary but I usually ask each individual for feedback after all the group suggestions have been made, including my own. I might ask, "What was said that seems most correct or true about you, or what was most meaningful to you?" It is often not my own comment which is chosen. When it is something that was suggested by several of the other participants, it is an encouraging experience for them as well.

At the end of this first group project I set aside time for sharing of each person's evaluation of the experience. I generally start it off by asking, "What did you learn about yourself or the others during this activity?* Is there any difference in how you feel at this moment, compared to how you felt when you walked in?"

I have discovered, repeatedly, that participants experience a dramatic change in mood after this carousel painting project. It is such a potent and stimulating exercise that the feeling which is usually reported is one of both exhilaration and complete relaxation.

Shared Responsibility

I believe that the impact of this project can at least in part be attributed to the experience of shared responsibility which enhances the participants' self-esteem. All group members, whether they are students in training or patients, have been exposed to the pressures of our society and its demands for excellence. In the process of concentrating on the task at hand, they feel a release from the fear of failure. By the time the session is over, there is no felt sense of personal inadequacy. The paintings are truly the product of a group effort. However, each individual is forced to struggle with his or her own reaction to this activity and to deal with any threatening feelings of anxiety or inferiority. "Am I going to be afraid of failing, or can I allow myself to be the beneficiary of my fellow worker's courage and cooperation?"

---

*Dreikurs routinely asked at the conclusion of the therapy session, whatever the mode of therapy, "What did you learn during this sesssion?" Dreikurs believes that all therapy is reeducation, education which replaces faulty learning (Dreikurs, 1960).

72

Holism

All the senses are involved in this carousel project. Each person listens to the music, visually experiences the colors, and has all the tactile sensations associated with holding the brush, dipping it, and stroking the paint onto the paper. Following this nonverbal activity, there is an opportunity to process verbally what has happened, so that participants can learn something about themselves. It is this experience of expressing one's unique holism* in a cooperative group effort which is extremely encouraging to participants. They feel so liberated from the pressures of society and fears of failure that they can again express the creativity with which we are all endowed. Since it is discouragement which is at the root of one's inability to function effectively, the exposure to such an encouraging situation is of vital significance.

Setting the Tone

I have found that this beginning project sets the tone for all subsequent sessions. The influence of ensuing activities is greatly enhanced, and they are much easier to present when group members have had this carousel experience first. Because their creativity has been released, participants can proceed further and further toward the goal of group unity and social interest through cooperation, without sacrificing the uniqueness of the individual or the development of individual potential.

PAINT ON THE SAME PAPER

Through a process of experimentation and innovation, it has been my experience that having two people paint on the same paper is the best activity to follow the carousel. At this time, forming relationships is the important step. This can be done in many ways, but my choice is to have two people work together. This project deals with such questions as: How sensitive am I to what goes on in other people? How much do

---

*Adler termed his psychology "individual," meaning that the person cannot be considered in parts or subsystems. We react as a whole to any situation, and we can only be understood in our entirety. In 1926 Smuts coined the term "holism." Adler stated that this term was what he meant by "individual" and felt that "holism" was less confusing to those unfamiliar with his psychology than his term "individual" (Adler, 1956).

73

I learn about other people from working with them? And what do I learn about myself through this process?

Instructions to the Participants

My instructions usually are, "Look around the room, select a person whom you hardly know or don't know at all, ask that person if he or she will work with you. Decide what kind of paper you want to use, select a large piece, then take that piece and two very small pieces with you to the table. Place the large paper in front of you. From this moment there is no communication, either by signs, gestures, or words. Then paint on the same paper.

"If one finishes before the other, do not in any way signal. Paint your immediate reaction to the situation on a small piece of paper, and when both have finished, hang up the two smaller pieces under the large sheet. Now when I say noncommunication I mean do not communicate. Do not look at each other or poke each other. Do not give any indication of your reaction or what you're painting, verbally or nonverbally."

Discussion

When all have finished, each couple talks about what was experienced during this period of painting. I ask, "What was your perception of this activity, and how did it go? What do you know about your partner that you did not know before, and what did you discover about your partner's reaction to this experience from what was painted on the small piece of paper?"

Interpretation

I find that the manner in which one proceeds to work in-dicates what the person has heard in the instructions. The in-structions are given explicitly. There is nothing said about work-ing together or cooperating. The partners pick each other and proceed to work as they perceive their own functioning in life situations, which is congruent with their family constellation. The child of a large family who has made his or her way in cooperative relationships is usually the one who moves first, often by reaching over to the partner's side of the paper to stimulate the other person into a cooperative painting effort. The person who is an only child may be very timid and continue to feel alone in the middle of the paper, hoping the other will make the first supportive move. There are as many varieties of examples seen in this exercise as there are creative expressions of the individual. How the participants find their way in their own family constellation is repeated in this exercise.

This is a very potent experience, because not only does one learn about the partner and how each perceives the other, but it is an experience showing how sensitive participants are to what goes on around them and to the intentions of their fellow workers. Are they aware of what's going on and what is expected of them, or are they completely oblivious? Are they willing to accommodate themselves to the situation, or do they revert to habitual patterns of functioning?

The Family Constellation

It is at this point that I give a brief outline of the theory of family constellation. I give examples of how children develop their unique line of movement in response to the perceived family atmosphere and relationships among family members. The possibilities open to each sibling will differ, according to the degree of cooperation and harmony versus competition and strife within the family. When possible I ask participants who are familiar with Adlerian psychology to discuss how they understand the theory of family constellation, and then I bring in whatever has not been said. When I started this project of having two people work together, I only had the one idea of demonstrating whether participants are sensitive to the other person's thoughts and desires and if they are willing to cooperate. The experience developed into something beyond the mere sensing and feeling, when I discovered that their responses were closely related to family constellation factors.

After the discussion of the large painting and the two smaller ones using the theory of family constellation, I often introduce a second, slightly different project. I again ask two people to paint on the same paper, but I select the people myself after observing how they work. In this instance the instructions are "One of you will paint first, and then the other one will continue." My choice might be to select a person who is very careless and even sloppy in execution, and a perfectionist, and ask the two to work together.

The Projects' Purpose

The purpose of this project is to change the habits or tone of the person's movement in the painting activity. One influences the other. The careless one loosens up the perfectionist, and the perfectionist encourages a certain amount of order in the one who is inclined to be careless. This becomes a dramatic learning experience when the partners discuss their different styles and how they felt about adjusting to the other's pattern.

It is sometimes very difficult to alter the partner's pattern, and a struggle may ensue. The one who is the perfectionist is often distressed by the carelessness of the other, and since they are permitted to speak to each other they can have a very heated argument like "Stop spoiling what I'm doing," or "Listen, why don't you loosen up and stop being such a square?"

This action makes for a lively discussion and frequently leads to much laughter, which is certainly an advantage. The first exercise promotes insight concerning patterns of functioning in life situations, and there's a tendency for participants to become quite introverted and to question, "Am I really like that?" This second activity breaks the tension of the first exercise and everyone laughs at themselves and each other, and how difficult it is to change the way they do things to conform to the needs of every situation.

As a rule, the session ends with people singing a song together. They feel relaxed and at ease after the experience of being first in a situation of complete concentration and then being open and free, sparring with each other like young bear cubs.

SELECTIVE LISTENING

I have discovered that one part of my instructions is frequently misunderstood, and I've often pondered at the wonder of this selective hearing. The hearing seems to be most selective in relation to my statement "Paint on the same piece of paper." As a rule, when I ask participants to recall what my instructions were, they repeat almost verbatim what I said until they come to this part. It is at that point where they hear what they want to hear, which is congruent with their movement in life.

It's puzzling to me why this simple statement is the one that is converted into what they want to hear. This is par-

76

ticularly true in foreign countries, when the translator doesn't translate quickly and goes astray by saying "paint together." I have to use great caution in my instruction to the translator: "Now please don't say paint together or change my words in any way. 'Paint on the same piece of paper' is what I wish to say." However, even in the English language, when there is no translation needed, this is frequently misunderstood.

Requesting Perceptions

A short time ago during a discussion of this project, something quite remarkable occurred. One large sheet of paper had two lines down the center, with a space in between, and the two partners had each painted on one side. I was curious about this separation and asked the first one, "What do you remember my saying in my instructions?" Everything was recalled exactly except when I said "paint on the same piece of paper." Instead of that she said, "Paint by yourself." I asked the other person, "What do you remember?" "Everything," she said, but when it came to that same part of the instructions, she said, "Do my own picture." "What is your family constellation?" "I can't really tell you because I have a twin sister."

Then I asked the first one, "What is your family constellation?"

"I'm also a twin, with no other children in the family." They had not known each other before but had nevertheless gravitated toward each other. We discussed the fact that twins are often so accustomed to being part of another person that they feel just part of a picture. They are not together—only part of. Occasionally they're so tired of being part of another that for once they want to be on their own. That was why they heard, "Paint by yourself, and paint your own picture." In each case they heard exactly what they wanted to hear, which fit into their movement in life according to their family constellation.

Participants who come from a large family in which the children had to cooperate, share, and make a place for themselves, usually choose someone who also comes from a large family and who related well with siblings. They will hear "Paint together" instead of painting on the same piece.

There are occasional isolates in the group, and then the selective hearing is "Paint by yourself, don't encroach on the other," or "Mind your own business."

I recall one case which was quite striking. Meta came from Australia. She had originally lived in South Africa, had married there at an early age, and had a very close relationship with her husband. They later moved back to Australia, but he died, and she came to Israel to see if she could live with her sister. I was presenting a workshop in Israel and they both came as participants. In the beginning of the session I had asked, as was usually my custom, how they all happened to come and what their interest was. Meta said, "I came because I am visiting here and I have a great deal of trouble communicating with people. I simply cannot make contact with anyone."

A Nonverbal Example

In this room I had an art therapist who was a friend of mine, and when it came time to choose partners for this activity, Thelma thought she could guide Meta into communication through nonverbal painting. She walked up to Meta and said, "Would you paint with me?" Meta was very happy to have someone approach her. Thelma then proceeded to paint huge stripes at the bottom and with her brush went over to Meta's side of the paper, giving her the message "Come and paint with me, I'm coming to you." Well, what did Meta do? She took a felt pen and painted a portrait at the bottom of the sheet, right in the center, and no matter how much Thelma came around her, Meta proceeded to paint only on this portrait.

When we talked about it later, I asked, "Thelma, what did you hear me say?" Thelma heard, "Paint on the same piece of paper." Then I asked Meta, "What did *you* hear me say?" She replied, "I didn't hear anything. I only knew that we were to do something, and I heard the part 'select the paper and paint with another person,' But I couldn't paint with her." "Meta, whose portrait is that?" She said, "My husband." The rest of the group said, "No, it's your portrait." And it was. It was a self-portrait, glasses and all. Then the group had a discussion. Meta does not wish to communicate with anyone. She still feels only a part of her husband, and indeed she painted herself, and she thought she was painting her husband, so she had joined him nonverbally and didn't want to have any communication with others. She said, "I didn't even see what Thelma was doing. I was just with my husband."

When they painted their small pictures, Thelma continued to reach over, but Meta left the paper blank. She painted nothing. There was no communication except the message "I don't want to have any part of anyone else. I just want to be with my husband." This was a difficult and powerful learning situation for her, because she had to face the fact that she actually didn't hear what I had said.

Building Upon Selective Hearing

Because of my experience with selective hearing in these instructions, I now use this project not just for the purpose of determining how sensitive participants are to what's going on in the other person but how they choose to hear what they want to hear, which I observe is in line with their family constellation and biased apperceptions. This can be one of the most effective learning experiences in art therapy.

DRAWING THE HANDS

I have found the following project to be fraught with many possibilities although it seems to be a very simple exercise. I ask the participants to take a piece of paper, use their hands as a model, and make an outline of their hands on the paper, using them in any way that they wish, to make a pattern from which they will later make a painting.*

The Self Is Revealed

It is very interesting to note the extent to which the inhibition of some people is revealed. For instance, one participant will take a hand and put it on one part of the paper, draw it, and will see no other possibility of using that hand. Another will turn it upside down, backwards, forwards, sideways, and keep drawing the hands, putting one hand on top of what they

---

*In Adlerian theory the hands are symbolically one's way of interacting with others. That's how we access the community. Drawing the hand is a representational pattern that transcends the ego. How are we willing to change the basic information of our hands without fear of losing ourselves, without concern for ourselves or moving beyond the basic form of the hand? If we change the hand into different formations to create a different effect, we're not so self-centered, so concerned that we have to stay with the basic pattern, and that bespeaks of security within the individual.

have already, so that they have a maze of patterns with which to work.

What the participant does with the outline reveals much about the self to each one. Do I see myself in a very simple, straightforward manner? Is my thinking so complicated that I confuse myself with this maze of patterns that I have painted, and then get lost in it? Do I stick to the outline and with the subject of hands, very meticulously outlining the hand, painting the fingernails, the veins and all the details? Do I disregard completely the fact that I've used my hand as a model and just look at the pattern that's formed and use this pattern for a creative, decorative design?

I remember one homicidal patient in the hospital painting the outline of his two hands on a black piece of paper, and then painting the hands red, with blood dripping on them, which was certainly expressing his homicidal tendency. It's very revealing to see the extent to which one thinks in a simple, straightforward manner, how complicated one is in one's thinking, how creative or how inhibited. At the same time it is an exercise that gives the leader the opportunity to help participants begin painting when they don't know what to do.

Use with Children

This is also a very good exercise to do with children, because they love to outline their hands. Their personality shows immediately. When they use the outline of their hands to create something else it's almost as if they were saying, "It is not important for me to remain as an individual. This one hand can be many other things."

Discussion

Following this painting activity, I ask each person to select one of the paintings and tell a story about it. What does this painting tell you? As group members we discuss what each picture means to them and what they see in it. Then I ask the individuals to talk about their own paintings and what their reaction is to what was said by the others.

We next have a discussion about where we are psychologically at this point: Are we willing to venture into something else, do we stay with the life patterns that are familiar to us? I know my hand, I recognize it, I do not want in any way to deface it. I know exactly what to expect of my hand, and I want to maintain the status quo. Are participants willing to submerge their hands, which would be reflections of their individual personalities, into something else for the sake of a new pattern or something which might evolve from what they're doing? It's a psychological discussion, actually, of "what are you like, what do you do and how do you move?" Actually, the original idea of using hands came from the well-known statement of Alfred Adler's: "If you really want to know a person, don't look at his mouth – watch his hands. See what he does with his hands."

Interpretations

I have recently experimented with a kind of free association technique during the discussion following this activity. I invite the group to respond to any possible symbolism in the paintings – to ask themselves, "Where do my hands guide me?" They are free to read into the paintings whatever they choose.

I recall that when I was in Israel in 1981, some very interesting interpretations were given for the same painting. One person observed that the hands looked as if someone were reaching out to be a part of the universe. Another person thought the hands were reaching out to touch a neighbor. A third group member felt that the hands were reaching into the "beyond," trying to understand what was unknown to them.

TEARING PAPER

Discovering the Method

One day at the hospital we were completely out of paper and had nothing on which to work. There were, however, many old paintings around. Out of this situation evolved a new project which I use with groups now but only rarely with hospitalized patients, depending on the level of confidence I have established with them.

The Procedure

I ask participants to select all the old paintings they don't like, and then everyone in unison tears them up into pieces. I say, "Select those paintings we've made so far that no one in the room cares for, that you don't like at all, and put those aside. Then tear them, tear them with great energy." In the case of children I would add, "Use your muscles and your strength, and really tear them with force." With adults, "If you can remember what makes you angry or can think of something in the past that bothered you, tear the paper with great vigor and destroy. When you have ripped them up completely, put everything in the center of the table." I sometimes give a demonstration and I cuss at times, "That-so-and-so bus driver didn't stop on time. That really makes me furious." Pow! and I tear the paper with great force.*

Then everyone takes several large sheets of paper and spreads them around the room or hangs them on the wall. In the hospital we spread the large papers on the wall because it's easier to pound, and the walking around, which is always good for patients, is encouraged because there is quite a little distance to go from one wall to another. I say, "Take the bits of paper you've torn and make piles of them in front of the huge pieces of paper. Take some paste and go from one to the other almost like a marathon, like a race of some kind, pasting a piece of paper on one and then going very quickly to the next sheet of paper. Keep slapping them on. Again, do it with vigor. Don't put the piece on gently. Hit it! Hit it really hard! Bump into each other, do anything. This is an activity of wild abandon. When you put this thing on the wall, after you've torn it with vigor, don't just pussyfoot around and put it on tenderly, but say, "POW, I've always wanted to hit _____, now I'm going to do it! Think of the things that you always wanted to do but didn't dare to do because you were so nice or such a good person."

Rebuilding

Once a participant pasted the piece of paper with great vigor and said, "I've always wanted to slap my mother-in-law, and this is the first time I can really experience this. There you have it!" and he slapped his paper on with gusto. It is

---

*You allow the person to maintain their uniqueness, but in expressing their anger they're making a contribution, so you've given them an antisuggestion (Adler, 1970). You've said, "Express your anger," and what you're telling them in actuality is "I want you to make a group contribution. In order to make this contribution you must with some vigor plaster this up there." They are unaware that from the very beginning they're contributing to the group.

an excellent way of helping participants express their anger, talk about it and act it out both verbally and physically.

I ask myself, "Now how does this fit with Adlerian theory?" I'm not too sure of the answer. Perhaps it gives people permission to be angry. In depression you don't talk about anger. You internalize it and it festers within you. You're too "good" to be angry. Here you don't have to be so good. People also have permission to be excited and run around, behaving in a way they may have always wished they could but never dared.

Adding Paint

If the activity gets out of hand, or when the papers are full, I will say, "Now let's go to the next step. Pull the paper so that the loose pieces fall off, sit back, and look at what you've done together. See if you can do anything to change the configuration of the collage with paint. Take a brush, paint around, in, on top or wherever you will, and see what you get out of it."

We then hang up the huge papers and discuss the activity. "Do you prefer the collage with or without the painting?" could be one question. "Why do you like it?" Asking what it makes the participant think of could be used as a projective test. "Can you tell us a story of what you see?"

Discussion

Ultimately we move to a discussion of the experience of first tearing up the papers and then building with the pieces. I might ask, "What do you think this project means? What reaction did you have? Did you feel angry, and if you did, what happened, and how do you feel now? Are you still so angry?" Or, "How do you resolve your anger, or did the activity dissolve it in any way?" Or, "Are you more angry than you were before, and do you want to talk about it?" Through the group's constructive effort, the ultimate realization comes that, "No matter how much I destroy I can always build it up again if I work with other human beings."

There are occasionally two or three participants who are so upset about having anything destroyed, and so cautious about offending or doing harm to anyone that they express trepidation related to this activity. They may say, "No, we have no right to destroy anything that anybody has created, even if the paintings have been discarded. I refuse to tear this up." If this contingency ensues I simply suggest tearing bits of paper, colored bits of paper, that haven't been used before. The only loss is the added attraction of the old paintings. In a setting other than a hospital, where scissors aren't available, one could use pieces of cloth or string or anything that can be superimposed on a sheet of paper to build up a collage.

The Difficulty of Facing Anger

One of my co-workers in the hospital didn't like this project at all. She actually did not want to be present when we were doing it because she felt it was too risky to undertake with a group of people who are hospitalized largely because of anger. She didn't feel she was in a position to deal with the situation herself since she had at one time been a patient, had a great deal of anger, and didn't want to experience it. Whenever I did this project she would ask to be excused, and wouldn't partake. She was one who, like many depressed people, couldn't tolerate destruction or express anger. In such cases, I respect the rejection of the project, and if the person is not in therapy with me, I don't go further with this. However, if a patient refuses, I will make a note of it so the therapist can follow through.

After this activity I often have participants do another small collage of their own. I say, "Take a small sheet of paper and do this one any way you want. You can do it with physical strength or you can do it passively, but build up on one sheet of paper your torn pieces of paper and see what you get out of it." This individual project tends to calm the group down. They become absorbed in rebuilding on their own, and at this point do not have to rely on the group. Creativity has been released and the uniqueness of each individual is apparent in the collages which result.

As a general rule, they have a satisfying experience planning and turning their own collage into something quite realistic. A child can turn it into a clown, for example. In a sense this activity is similar to the carousel in that participants first share and then do their own. It's the same sequence except that this one involves physical force, energy, and the venting of anger and the carousel does not.

Cooperation

The purpose of this tearing paper project is largely to express anger through destruction, to verbalize and physically express it, and then to experience the constructive group effort of building something up again. No matter how much you destroy, you can build again if you cooperate with a group. You can create beauty out of chaos. Nothing is really destroyed or lost that can't be restored if a group of people are willing to work together.

PAINTING EARLY RECOLLECTIONS

Dynamic Symmetry

Psychological theory is clarified and becomes more meaningful to me if I translate it into a visual pattern. In my early training as a painter I studied the old masters, who composed their paintings on the basis of dynamic symmetry. All the peripheral subject matter converged on a golden circle which was the central focus of the painting. Take, for example, da Vinci's painting of the Annunciation. What he wanted us to see is the face of the Virgin Mary. Therefore, everything in the painting leads the eye to that point, through vertical, diagonal and horizontal lines. It is the face that makes the sharpest and most important impression on the viewer.

I think of this principle of dynamic symmetry when soliciting early recollections* in art therapy. "What do you remember

---

*Alfred Adler used early recollections as a diagnostic tool in therapy. Early recollections reflect the individual's present stance toward the world. The early recollection includes the fictive (because it demands perfection which is impossible) goal that people think would give them a place in this world if they were to achieve it. It includes their view of other people and the world, moral and ethical beliefs, the path to their goal, and their self-concept. The particular goal also defines how people "should" be, the "self-ideal." Early recollections support one's present view of life. The attitudes and movement which we now display are supported by our early recollections. Whenever we desire proof that the world is really made up in the way that we suppose, we merely call forth a recollection which supports that view. The recollections, which we clearly visualize and remember distinctly today, may never have actually occurred, though it would be difficult to convince the recollector that this may be so. We reconstruct our past (early recollections) to fit our current life situation.

For additional reading related to early recollections see: Dreikurs, R. and Mosak, H. "Adlerian psychotherapy," in *Current Psychotherapies*, edited by Corsini, R. Itasco, Ill.: Peacock, 1972, pp. 35-83; and Mosak, H. On Purpose. Chicago: Alfred Adler Institute, 1977.

85

from early childhood? What is now clear in your memory?" It is the visualization which is the kernel of the recollection. Everything else is the embellishment and the movement leading toward the actual memory. Early recollections support the lifestyle, and one can call on these supports to reinforce and fortify the lifestyle at will.

Procedure

When I use early recollections with a group, one member tells an early memory while the others listen. Everyone then paints that early recollection and puts themselves into the recollection visually, showing how they would have reacted in that situation.* My instructions are, "Listen very carefully to what you hear, and then paint what you remember, and put yourself in that situation as if it were your own early recollection." I give no other instructions.

Finding a Solution

The one who has given the early recollection is asked to choose among all the subsequent paintings the one which offers the most pleasing alternative to the recollection. However, this person often paints the memory differently from how it was originally told, and thereby discovers a better solution without any outside help at all.

There is a stronger tendency to see one's own solution when visualizing the problem than when verbalizing it. It is quite dramatic to see how the person who tells the early recollection works out a better alternative to the problem when confronted with it visually. In my experience this has not happened when only the verbal approach is used.

An Example

The first time I tried using early recollections this way, a man told the following story. "We lived in a small country town and in the neighboring town was a new shopping center. My mother was very excited about going to the shopping center so that she could visit all the new shops. She said I could

---

*I am indebted to Mika Katz, Tel Aviv, Israel, for this technique which she uses verbally in groups and which I have adopted for use with painting.

86

come with her and take my little red wagon. It was a beautiful day. There were wonderful shops with striped awnings and mountains in the distance. I was dragging my wagon and Mother was holding my hand as we walked along the wooden sidewalk. Beside the walk there was a nice patch of grass on a small hill. As we approached a place in the walk where a board was broken, my mother left me to go and look in a shop window. I was terrified. There I stood, petrified, afraid that I would fall into the hole and there was no one to help me."

At this point the people in the room painted what they remembered from this recollection, putting themselves into it as directed. Surprisingly, the man who had given the recollection painted himself rolling down the grass instead of standing there terrified. He suddenly realized that he knew how to take care of himself and didn't need to depend on Mother to rescue him. Since he was at that time in therapy to work out his dependence on a woman, this revelation was very meaningful to him.

Another Example

Another's recollection: "I think I was probably not more than two and a half years old, and I was standing in my crib screaming because I was all alone. I was terrified because I was afraid my mother wouldn't come to get me. Suddenly I heard her coming on the staircase, and I was even more petrified because I had messed my bed and I didn't want her to see it."

I asked, "What do you remember most clearly?'

"I remember that I wanted somehow not to have her see that I had messed my bed, that this awful thing had happened."

When he painted his recollection he eliminated the mess completely. It was a perfectly clean bed. He was still crying for his mother but happy that she was going to come and get him. He decided he didn't have to dwell on his mistakes but could forget about them and go on with life.

There were many variations of the situation painted by the rest of the group. One very outgoing, expansive woman painted wallpaper, furniture, a vase of flowers, and covered up the mess with a colorful blanket. She stood there with outstretched arms just laughing and waiting for her mother. Another variation included the participant's favorite doll, Raggedy Ann, on the floor, also petrified and crying, so she had a companion in her fear and didn't feel as alone.

In the discussion following the painting activity, as is my usual procedure, I asked if he liked the alternative solution he had found for himself, or if there were any other paintings of different solutions that he preferred or with which he would like to experiment. The other solutions reflect how each participant would have behaved in that situation and usually represent a variety of possible alternatives, some of which will be more positive than others.

Use with Psychotic Patients

Even psychiatric patients can come up with good solutions. Although they are putting themselves into the recollection and the way they do this will reflect their own troubled state of mind, they may have more courage to experiment with alternatives because it is not their original recollection.

With psychotic patients I would recommend using more than one recollection for each participant and making the process more like group therapy in the following way. After everyone paints one recollection I would have the same person continue with perhaps four recollections, telling each one and having all group members paint each one, putting themselves into it in every case. It may take a whole session for each person, so it would be a lengthy process. When all the paintings are completed and we can see a pattern in the recollections I would have the subject choose from the alternatives which were painted. "What would you like to work on? Which of your basic mistakes do you want to concentrate on first?"

In addition to working with the person who has given the recollections, the other participants, as they put themselves into each one in painting, are working on their own predicaments. The discussion can be focused on them also. "Do you see an answer to your current problem in what you have just worked out for someone else?"

Care Is Necessary

It's important not to let the participants off the hook by asking them to paint a different solution, although some may selectively hear me say this when I'm asking them to put themselves into the situation. They may not want to expose themselves and therefore may not hear what I'm actually saying. I am very careful not to give additional directions or to structure the painting in any way other than to give the instructions already stated.

I suggest that this early recollections project be used judiciously and only by Adlerians who have had training in the interpretation and use of early recollections. I would also limit its use to situations in which it is possible to follow up with psychotherapy on an individual or group basis. This exercise can reveal the lifestyle dramatically to an extent beyond the point where some patients are ready to work. They need the support of psychotherapy.

PAINT AS A CHILD

Once in Switzerland too many people registered for my workshop, so I volunteered to give four hours extra to the remaining twelve. Most were students, 30 or under, without painting experience. I planned to do the carousel activity with them, ask them to paint their own picture, and then discuss how all of human behavior reflects the stance one takes in life.

A Change of Plans

A peculiar thing happened at the beginning of the session. The oldest person in the group said, "I don't really know what I'm doing here. This is for kids." At this point I changed my plan and said to the group, "Would you be willing to paint something that you liked to paint as a child, and in the same manner?" They all did this, and for two of them it was a dynamic experience, suggesting an early recollection which helped to clarify their own movement and mistaken goals.

Rebecca

One of the participants took a huge sheet of paper to paint on, instead of the smaller piece which I had indicated was appropriate. When the others were all done and it was time for discussion, I spoke to her. "Rebecca, do you mind if we start to talk while you continue to paint, since we have very little time?" She threw down her brush in anger and put her painting up on the wall, as the others had done. I turned to her first. "Rebecca, tell us about your painting."

She had painted a broad field of green, a Tyrolean house, and in just one corner she had started painting tiny flowers. She said, "I love to go to my summer house every year with my family. It's beautiful there and I love the green grass and the house. I used to paint a picture of it after I came back home, but as soon as I'd get to the flowers my teacher would say, 'Stop painting. You don't have enough time.' Now you did the same thing to me."

Rebecca believes authority figures stop her and prevent her from doing what she wants. In this case, even though the rest of the group was not trained in Adlerian thinking, they understood the self-fulfilling prophecy which was evident in her behavior. "Why did you select such a big piece of paper?" they asked.

Ruth

Another participant, Ruth, had chosen rose colored paper and had painted a beautiful Christmas tree with wonderful ornaments, a glowing fireplace, and at one end of the room a tall, slender girl in a white robe walking out. Following my usual procedure, I asked her to tell the group about what she had painted and why she had painted this as a child.

Ruth responded, "Christmas in our house was the most joyous time of the year and I was so very happy when Christmas came. The Christmas child came to our house to decorate the tree and she is just about to leave. Every year I painted this because it was such a happy time in our house. For weeks after I'd keep painting this picture at school because – oh, no, it wasn't a happy time! I always wanted some gold paint for a crown on the Christmas child's head and silver paint to use for slippers on her feet. I never had the gold or silver paint and I didn't have it today, and I'm *not* happy!" This recollection clearly indicates Ruth's conviction that life could be so beautiful but there is always something missing in it for her.

A New Project—Often Fruitful

When this exercise evokes early recollections, as in these two cases, it becomes a very fruitful experience. However, this project occasionally falls flat on its face. Participants sometimes paint what they think they remember as children but in truth are not painting as they did at that time, but as they would

90

in the present, with their lack of painting skill. If the therapist is experienced in art and is knowledgeable about children's painting, the difference is discernible.

Because of the serendipitous success of this project, largely as a result of the early recollections it evoked, I have added it to my usual sequence of activities and now use it regularly.

PAINTING BLIND

This activity evolved from my own questions about the nature of painting. I have wondered what it is about painting which produces so many different sensations. Is it primarily a visual or a tactile experience? Moving a brush on the paint evokes a reaction which is different from that experienced when painting with one's fingers, and the colors themselves create a strong visual impact. After discussing with my daughter, Eva Dreikurs Ferguson, how to test some of my ideas, I decided to have art therapy participants try painting as if they were blind. I experimented first with an international group of professionals who were learning my methods, and did not use music at all.

Directions

I merely said to the group, "Choose a piece of paper. Tear it in two. Put one part on the floor and the other on the table. After one minute, during which you can prepare yourself, I will say, 'Shut your eyes, you are blind.' If you open your eyes during the activity, please stop painting and do not look at what you've been doing. When you're ready, open your eyes, put this paper under the table, again without looking at it, take the other piece and paint on it with your eyes open."

Participants' Responses to This Problem-Solving Task

It was amazing to watch how these people reacted. One man from Denmark quickly made a ball out of paper towels, put in it the center of his paper, chose three colors and put them in a row in front of him, numbering them as he marked their places so that he'd know what color he was using. He proceeded to use the wad of paper as a guide and painted out from it in concentric circles.

Another put four little pieces of paper at each corner and painted in toward the center. A rather timid German lady surrounded her paper with a barricade of paint jars and other objects, so that no one could encroach on her territory, and she would not paint over the edges. One man kept sniffing his paper so that he could tell where it was damp and therefore already covered, and another held his hand close to the paper to feel the location of the dampness.

Observing reactions to this vulnerable situation, it suddenly occurred to me that the activity was in fact a problem solving test. How will they face this task with the loss of their visual sense? Two gave up immediately and opened their eyes. They lacked the courage to proceed without vision.

A Sample of Life Patterns

I now use this project as a technique to demonstrate the varied manner in which people respond to the unexpected tragedies of life. It could also be used to illustrate reactions to being suddenly handicapped in real life. Some withdraw, some use it as an excuse, others overcome it, and the response always reflects the individual's general life pattern. The pampered child, for instance, is accustomed to being served and hasn't developed the courage to overcome obstacles.

A Suicidal Patient

Once when I was involved in this project with a group of psychiatric patients, although I don't usually attempt this with new or apprehensive hospitalized groups, a nurse brought in a woman and handed me a note which read, "This new patient is suicidal. Don't leave her alone, and if you are able to discuss suicide, please do."

I had no idea how I was going to do this, but when we began to paint, she refused to participate, saying, "I'd rather be dead than blind." I then had a perfect opportunity to discuss suicide with the entire group. I asked each one, "Under what circumstances would your rather be dead?" We talked about why people want to give up and commit suicide, the controlling aspect of suicide, the lack of cooperation (i.e., "If I can't have all my faculties I am angry with life and would rather die than adjust to it"), and a timid versus courageous movement through life.

A Rebellious Patient

Another person sat down and refused to paint because she felt it was unfair to be asked to do something for which she had not been trained. She complained that if one doesn't have vision one wouldn't be painting and therefore the project was silly. Her rebellious attitude became quite clear. "Things must be just so; otherwise I don't play the game" was her private logic.

Liberation

During the discussion period, participants have the opportunity to describe how they felt while painting with their eyes shut. One common theme, especially among professionals, is one of liberation. They often report a sense of freedom, or of relief, as if being blind absolved them of responsibility and they could do anything without fear of failure. Some discover through this experience that they have been comparing themselves to others and evaluating their own performance in real life more than they realized. They had thought themselves free, but in fact this was a delusion. It was only when they actually couldn't see what other people were doing that they felt free.

An Idiosyncratic Rhythm

Participants themselves are often amazed at the similarity between what they did with their eyes closed and later with them open. There seems to be an idiosyncratic rhythm which is expressed in each individual's work, regardless of the handicap imposed by this project. In fact, if there is no similarity between the two, I suspect it's because the person has peeked at the first painting before starting the second. If they consciously try to improve on what was done first, the natural creative rhythm is interrupted. Efforts to control the situation only interfere with the result.

MURAL PAINTING

The First Project

There are two projects which I introduce towards the end of a series of sessions that involve mural painting and which test one's ability to work in a group. The origin of painting together as a group goes back to the early days when I worked with juvenile delinquents, turning deviant into positive behavior by putting the destructive leaders in charge of a group so that their energy was used constructively to create a mural.

I now do group murals in several ways. I prefer to start by asking the group to divide themselves into small groups, the number in each group ranging from three to five depending upon the size of the total group. I ask each small group to get together, choose the size of paper, and work on the same sheet of paper, painting a mural. Those are the only instructions for the first project.

Discussion

One of the first questions that I ask in the discussion which follows is, "How did you choose each other? Why did you choose to work together?" I often find that people are attracted to allies or competitors. There are many possible answers, and the final product usually indicates what ensued during their experience. For instance, I often ask the whole group to react to a mural, saying, "What kind of an effort do you think this was?" The response might be, "It looks as if there was a struggle," or, "It looks like a cooperative effort," or, "It is completely chaotic and it's difficult to tell what went on." The next step is to ask each person in the group how they perceived what happened. "Why did you join this group? What happened in the group while you were painting?"

An Example

The most striking incident that I can remember happened in one of my earliest art therapy sessions, when a mural indicated a great deal of conflict. I was working with a group who were from the same industrial organization and were actually on the board of directors together. This group had been having a hard time working together, and when I started out by saying, "Take a huge sheet of paper and four of you paint a mural," there was immediate chaos.

Two of the four immediately decided to quarrel with each other. The conversation went something like this: "You're behaving in the same way that you always do with me. When we have a meeting with the board you never listen to me. You ride roughshod over me, and you did that when we were painting. No matter what I put on the paper you disregarded it and effaced it and had your own way every minute of the time."

94

The other two participants withdrew from the struggle and later put one or two little strokes here and there. It was interesting to find that of the two who withdrew, one was a second child who could not compete with a stronger, older sibling and would just withdraw, and the other was a middle child who was engulfed by two siblings and withdrew when there was any struggle in the family. They behaved exactly the same way in the mural painting when they were confronted with two people who were in a struggle for dominance.

Sibling Position

The two contenders who were struggling during this mural painting, one feeling that the other was railroading her and pushing her aside, were each the oldest child in the family and had a dominant position. They met head on in a collision course because they each wanted to have their own way and wouldn't give way to the other one.

I asked if this experience was similar to the problems they were having in their board meetings. The response from one was, "That's exactly what happens. As soon as I open my mouth, she stops me and doesn't let me proceed, and that's what she did in our painting."

The Second Project

At this point I introduced the second project which I'll describe now. I ask the same groups to paint another mural together but not to paint anything until they come to an agreement. "This time do not paint anything unless you know what you're going to do, how you're going to go about it, and what your goals are. Do not paint at all if you cannot reach agreement. The important part is to reach agreement — not a compromise. If you compromise, you'll behave in your usual manner. You'll step aside and say, 'After you.' If any time during your painting you feel that the agreement has been broken, please stop and come to a new decision."

In the example above, when the two people who fought so violently really talked things out and came to an agreement, they came up with an important and constructive mural. They were very happy to find that they could work together harmoniously, that they could understand what the intention of the other person was, and they planned to follow through in their future board meetings to see if they couldn't be more effective in what they were doing. It was very enlightening to look at the two murals. There was no comparison between what they did when they had an agreement, however loose or imcomplete, and what they did before, without an agreement.

A Method of Problem Solving

This technique could be used as an opener for any kind of large organizational meeting when there is an agenda to follow which involves potential strife. Before proceeding with the agenda, members can come to an agreement, through painting, about how to proceed. Then perhaps the regular meeting can follow in a more peaceful way with the business at hand getting done, because the differences have already been talked out and the procedure decided on.

The two murals were a striking demonstration that a group needs to be in agreement in order to be productive. For business meetings this means agreement on agenda, on time, and especially an agreement to stop the meeting as soon as members start shouting at each other, and resume at another time.

Family Constellation Factors

Some of the groups painted together without any struggle, and the family constellation would indicate that they had learned how to accommodate their desires to the welfare of the group early in life and so felt quite comfortable in this situation. I have only had one instance when a group came to me and said, "We can't paint together. We simply cannot come to an agreement." The other people had practically completed their murals, and this group was still arguing and fighting. My response was, "Okay, you have solved your problem. You know that you are a group of people who can't come to an agreement. Now let us see why you can't." We looked at their family constellations to help explain how difficult it was for them to step out of the roles they had learned in childhood, even for this project. All four of them wanted to dominate the situation and were therefore not able to come to an agreement.

After both projects are completed, I begin the discussion by asking, "How do you perceive what happened? Did you at any time during the group feel that the agreement was broken? And if you did, what did you do about it, or why didn't you take action? Are you accustomed as the middle child always to fit into the situation and let your big sister and little brother have their way? What kept you from saying, 'Let's stop. We've broken the agreement'? Did you have discussion all the way through? Did you learn anything about yourself in the course of doing this? Did you learn anything about your reactions to the other people in the group? Do you know anything more about the people you worked with than you knew before? If so, what is it that you know about them as individuals that you didn't previously?"

Generalizing

After this project, as I do with all others, I ask, "Now how does what you experienced here apply to your life situation and how you function in your family, in your office, or in your school? How was this experience similar or different? What have you learned here which could help you in your daily lives? That's the real issue. It's possible that you're thinking, 'I'm not a painter. I can't really express myself,' or 'Well, I'm just taking a course now. This doesn't mean anything!' " In most cases the painting situation is no different from what happens in their lives generally. When you pin it down and say, "How does this resemble your everyday living?", you can then point directly to how people behave as whole human beings no matter what the situation.

Discussion

In the discussion period, participants share their reactions to the experience, and I help them understand why they responded as they did, using family constellation theory. "Let's stop a minute and investigate why you did this." We might, for example, discuss a woman who was a second-born child with a very strong, domineering sister or brother and, since there was no way of winning in this situation, stepped aside and did nothing. This person didn't hold her ground and say, "Now stop a minute, we have not lived up to our agreement. This isn't what we were going to do." I then point out how participants reenact the role that they had as children and which they still have as adults in their relationships with other people.

Selecting Partners

In the introduction to these projects I would suggest that if participants painted together as a couple before and had any struggle or difficulty, it might be advisable to paint together again on the mural for which an agreement is necessary. However, if they would like to change and paint with other people just to see what the experience is like, they are free to choose.

It is ultimately the participants' choice with whom to work on each of these murals. They may choose to paint together because they've already enjoyed painting with each other and want to continue. The only suggestion I make is that they stay together to paint the mural with agreement if they have previously been struggling.

An Example

I explain that people are often attracted to each other without knowing why, and I use Dreikurs' example of the couple who meet at a party, the handsome man and the darling little girl, who immediately fall in love. Here is this great, big, heroic human being who always took care of his darling baby sister, and here is a baby sister who has looked up to her big brother, or strong father, and now here he is – and it's love at first sight. They get married, and it's a beautiful relationship, until a year is over and the man thinks, "Why doesn't she make her own decisions once in a while? I'm tired of waiting on her. It's really a pain in the neck." She says, "Why is he such a bully? Why doesn't he occasionally let me do what I want?" Similarly, the characteristics which attract participants to each other in the beginning, as they look at each other in this room, are the same things they fight about when they're painting together. Something in their lifestyles draws them together.

Leadership

The group dynamics vary according to the number painting in each group. It's quite different when three are working together as opposed to five. The group of three is more likely to continue to work together on the second project. In a group of five, it's much easier for one or two to drop out, because there is usually a leader who takes over verbally or nonverbally.

Most groups respond well to leadership, and if there's a strong leader there's usually at least one passive group leader who loves to be served, and who is delighted to stand back and say, "Oh, yes, that's beautiful. I like what you did. Please go ahead." These people let the leaders take over, which is acceptable because it's done by agreement. The important element is seeing clearly how they function with other people, here and in their daily lives. Many configurations emerge in the discussion. "Was there a leader in your group? Who was it? Did you feel the leadership? Did you like it? What was the leader's role?"

An Example

Many years ago in Israel, a very meek, mild looking young man was working with three women, and when we started to discuss this activity I asked each person, "How do you perceive it went, and what did you do?" He replied, "Well, we agreed on the paper, we agreed on what we were going to paint, everybody was in complete agreement, and we started. Then I felt Rifka telling me what to do and what not to do and pushing me aside, and I just simply stopped painting." "Why?" "Rifka reminds me of my older sister who always did this to me, and I never could withstand her pressure. So rather than suffer again, I just let her have her way."

Self-Understanding

It seems to happen time and time again, that in a group of four there is an antagonist from which one group member withdraws, as he or she withdrew as a child. In discussion it can be brought out how this person still withdraws from conflict situations rather than resolves them. All participants gain some awareness of their own movement in life.

Setting the Tone

There's usually someone in each group who sets the tone for the project. If it's a strong leader who dominates the situation, the other partners have little chance, but if it is a constructive leader, then what ensues is a very harmonious and beautiful painting, because members have accepted the leadership without resentment. The constructive leader is usually one who has been the mediator of the family while growing up – the one who saw to it that everything ran smoothly, and took the lead in this regard.

Beauty Follows Agreement

The sequence of these two projects, first without specific instructions and secondly with agreement, brings out something very interesting from an artistic point of view. It is hard to believe that paintings which are the end product of something that's completely cerebral, when you talk over every inch of the way and paint only if there's agreement, can still be so spontaneous and beautiful. It is contrary to how we always think of creativity. We tend to think that if you plan something you lose its beauty and charm, its flow and spontaneity. One would think any possibility of creative painting would be ruined, but this is not so.

The paintings that are done with agreement have a great sense of beauty, more so than the early ones when there had been fighting, and no less than those done by groups who have not struggled at all. They have a continuity, a rhythm, and a sense of composition. One can conclude that the joy of agreeing with one's fellow being, and working out a project together, is satisfying in terms of both relationship and the end result, and is worth the slight sacrifice of originality. These projects prove how difficult it is to come to an agreement, how we have suffered by not working together in harmony, and the beauty which is produced when we do.

FULFILLMENT, FRUSTRATION AND THE MAGIC PILL

Control and Avoidance of Responsibility

These are two projects which are related to control and avoidance of responsibility. Since I don't use these activities at the beginning of a series of sessions, many participants have already increased their painting skills and can express themselves amazingly well in these projects despite the fact that the majority have never had any previous art experience. Having been released from the anxiety of success or failure during earlier group sessions, they have learned to use their brush and materials efficiently enough to paint what they want.

The Projects

Each participant is asked to paint two paintings, the first one showing what fulfills their lives and the second showing what frustrates them. I am aware that most of the participants are not yet skilled enough to paint the realistic subject matter that they would like in this project. Therefore I suggest that "It does not have to be a realistic portrayal of fulfillment or frustration. It can be a symbolic one, and you will have the opportunity to tell us what your symbolism stands for." This reduces the anxiety.

The Discussion

After they have painted both pictures, I ask them to hang them up, the one of fulfillment above the one that frustrates. In spite of my instructions, some express their own unique line of movement by electing to hang their paintings in a different arrangement. For example, one woman once hung hers in the opposite way, explaining, "Even when I'm happy, my frustration is always with me. It's part of my life and I can't escape it."

I ask the participants, one at a time, to talk about their two paintings, and I ask the group, "Do you have similar experiences that are fulfilling?" They all have a chance to discuss common experiences or situations which lead to feelings of personal fulfillment. When we discuss what frustrates each one I will ask the group, "Now what else could 'Carol,' for example, do in such a situation?" The discussion turns into an exchange of alternative ideas for easing the frustration.

While there is often some similarity of form or specific content among paintings, almost without exception fulfillment is expressed through a natural setting: a stream, an ocean, a tree — rarely cities. It seems that people feel embedded in nature and have a desire for the peace of nature and want to go back to it. It is easy to start a discussion by saying, "What do you see that you all have in common in your paintings?" The usual commonality is a desire for the peace, tranquility, beauty and grandeur of nature.

The specific frustrations vary among individuals, but the common denominator that emerges strikingly reflects the era in which we live. The general theme is "People simply do not behave the way I would like them to behave," or "I cannot control this situation. Things are beyond my control. I can't

101

deal with them. It is taken out of my hands." For instance, "How can I release political hostages?" Or, "How can I stop wars?" "How can I get the ERA passed?" The pervading, all-encompassing pattern of loss of control is a reflection of the world in which we live. World tensions have a great influence on the individual's frustration. I ask the whole group, "What do you have in common that frustrates you?" And they can readily see the common thread.

The individual frustrations expressed in their paintings are often ideas such as "I wish I could get myself to go on a diet," or "I wish I could get my mother-in-law to stop interfering with the children." Through group discussion, participants have a chance to confront what it is that fulfills them and what frustrates them, and how they can bring the two together to make them more congruent.

At this point I'd like to reassure the reader that human beings are not completely out of control. We can always change the situation through constructive activity rather than trying to control it. "What can I do about the situation rather than how can I control it" would be the point of my discussion with participants after this project.

Freedom from Responsibility

Experiencing fulfillment in nature, away from the city and away from the stress of immediate life situations, must have a fictitious quality. "If I were somewhere else, then I could meet my problems. It's only because I am here that I can't face up to the situation. If I lived in a peaceful, tranquil place, then I would get along so well with my children, with my husband, that my problems would disappear and the world would be a better place." These are the mistakes of the lifestyle "IF ONLY." If only I were somewhere else, then life would be beautiful and I would be able to do something else about the problems. It isn't only because nature is beautiful, but I wonder why there is this common denominator of fulfillment in nature. It has an escape quality.

I experimented one day with an idea for a project and discovered that this one also brought to light the longings that individuals have in common, and their predisposition to avoid life tasks.* Eight patients and three staff people were present in the hospital group. I said, "I'm going to give you a magic pill and ask you to swallow this pill.** You will be wherever you want to be. Now paint this place where you'd choose to be."

The three staff members painted Switzerland because I was about to depart for Switzerland and they dearly wanted to go with me. But every one of the eight patients painted Las Vegas—the strip, the gambling tables, the floor show, everything about Las Vegas. My question was, "Have you ever been to Las Vegas?" "No." "Have you seen anything on TV recently about Las Vegas?" "No." "Well, why are you all painting Las Vegas?" The common theme that emerged from the discussion was "I can get something without working for it. By myself and with my own efforts I'll never be able to amount to anything. What I need is one stroke of luck and I will be rich, and for the rest of my life I will be able to just enjoy myself. Look at all the fun I can have and I won't even have to pay for it." The general idea was "I can have something for nothing and I won't have to do a thing because, first of all, I'm not able to do anything, I'm not capable of doing anything, and secondly, this is just going to be a joy ride."

Of all of the times I've done this magic pill project, I have never had anyone paint the room where we were working as a place where they'd like to be. This puzzles me, because the feedback I get so often is "I feel so fine here, I feel so relaxed, I feel so wonderful." Now if this is so, why do they want to be somewhere else? Perhaps there is a misunderstanding of the directions. Since I do give them a magic pill, they think they must go somewhere else, and it doesn't occur to them that they might not want to be anywhere else.

PAINTING AN ASSIGNMENT

Toward the end of the series of sessions either in the hospital with patients or a semester course, or in a series of art therapy

---

*Adler (1958) believes that when anyone is experiencing emotional maladjustment there is always present a desire to escape from the responsibilities of life: getting along with others, work, and love.

**The magic pill technique has many uses in Adlerian therapy. Whatever the undesirable situation which would be cured by the pill, that is the situation in which the individual is avoiding responsibility (Dreikurs, 1961).

workshops, when participants have already been working with me for 20 to 30 hours, I write assignments on slips of paper and pass them out to each participant, indicating a specific painting subject.

I write down a series of subjects, such as a city, a forest, the interior of your kitchen—whatever comes to my mind. I don't even coddle participants by assigning simple projects that I think they'll be able to carry out easily. Then I pass these out randomly. I do not do it selectively in any way. However, there are times when I do give a choice. If I see people with a look of wonderment on their faces as if they are saying, "How am I going to do this? I don't like this assignment at all," I will sometimes say, "If you don't like your assignment and would rather have another, see if you can trade it with someone else in the group who doesn't like theirs either." This negotiating works out well but doesn't often happen. There's not much changing of assignments because most have gotten to the stage where they are not concerned with perfection. They are courageous enough to make the effort no matter what the result, because they have already experienced my nonjudgmental approach to art therapy, in which there are no rights and wrongs.

A Test

This is a test of the participants' courage. Are they willing at this point to paint a subject that they are assigned even if they do not feel capable of carrying it out realistically because of their lack of skill? Are they willing to do it imperfectly and express what I have asked them to express, or are they still inhibited by perfectionism and will refuse the assignment? Some will either not do it at all or do it symbolically, explaining, for example, "I couldn't really paint a farm, so this is what a farm seems like to me. It has in it all the thoughts I have about a farm." This exercise demonstrates the participants' willingness to take a chance.

Asking participants to paint an assignment also indicates to me whether or not they are willing to accept instructions and follow what is asked of them. Some may still be rebellious. It is especially enlightening to see if those teenagers who are defying authority have gotten to the point where they can accept an assignment or if they still have the attitude, "I do what I do when and how I want." I use this activity as an examination to see how far along the participants are in the course of their experience with me. It indicates clearly whether or not they have changed their attitudes toward a work situation, or a life task, so that they can contribute without evaluating their performance.

Discussion

After the painting we discuss the experience. I ask each participant, "What was your assignment, and how do you like what you did?" After this interchange I ask the group, "Why do you think I did this? What do you think is the purpose of this project?" After their comments I quite frankly explain, "My purpose was to learn where you are at this point in your experience with me. Are you willing to accept an assignment? Are you rebelling against it? Do you feel courageous enough to carry out an assignment for which you do not feel skillfully able? Are you willing to do an abstract or a symbolic picture of what I have asked, or are you rebellious and refuse to work at all? This is what I wanted to determine."

I often go on to say, "Now there are possibly some of you who have shown rebellion in what you have done. Can the group pick out those paintings which show resistance? What was the subject matter, and what did the person paint?" We usually have the rebellion demonstrated clearly in the kind of symbolic painting that one might expect – agitated strokes, undecipherable, unrecognizable objects, sometimes superimposed bits of colors that are hard to distinguish – those sorts of things that would express, "I won't let you even guess what I'm trying to do because I'm not about to accept your assignment."

Use with Psychiatric Populations

With a psychiatric patient population, the sequence may not work as well. Patients don't always stay long enough to attain the level of encouragement necessary to do this activity. If patients are new it may be much more difficult for them to accept the assignment. When I hand it to a new patient I might well give the comfort of saying, "Perhaps this will be a little difficult for you because the rest of us have worked together before, so do whatever you want with it. And you may choose not to do it at all if you wish." They typically choose to do it anyway.

I remember a psychotic patient who came into the group one day when the subject was "paint a forest, any kind of forest – a realistic, an imaginary, winter, summer, spring, or any kind of forest you like." They were all happily painting a forest when the nurse brought Sue in, and she just sat there. I said, "Sue, we are painting a forest today. You see, at the table there we have colored papers. Would you be kind enough to get up and select a piece of paper and bring it back and paint?" She just sat, and I thought, well, I've got to get her moving somehow. I went over to her and touched her elbow to see if she would pull back or just react passively. I said, "Come with me, Sue," and I guided her by the elbow over to the paper. I said, "Select a piece of paper." She just stood in the same position. I thought perhaps she couldn't decide. Therefore, I took three pieces of paper and said, "Take one of them," which she did, to my amazement. I said, "Let's go back to the table." No movement. Again I touched her arm, and there was no resistance. She walked back to the table, and just stood. With her elbow I eased her down and she sat. I put the paper in front of her and gave her three jars of paint.

"Select one color with which to paint, and then take a brush and use that one color. Put the brush in the paint, and paint anything. You don't have to paint a forest. Just get the feel of what the paint is like." There was no response – nothing. So again I put the brush in her hand and said, "Dip the brush in the paint." Nothing. I took her hand, dipped the brush in the red, and swished it, and stopped. "Sue, wash the brush." No movement. I lifted her hand, put it in the water, washed the brush, wiped it with the towel. "Sue, put it in the yellow now."

No response. Again, hand in yellow, another stroke. "Now, wash your brush." No movement. I did this again, until I had used the three colors, and then I just left her and walked away. To my great surprise she proceeded to work. She continued to put the brush in, and make strokes, agitated strokes, but she continued to work. When it was time to put the paintings on the wall, she put hers up. The other patients said, "Sue, that's so nice what you did. We like it. It's not a forest but we like what you did." She just stood there, not quite as rigid as she was before.

It was time to continue. I had asked the rest of the patients at that point to paint anything that they'd like to paint for the end of the period, and I asked Sue what she would like to do, and to my surprise she said, "I want to do a forest." It was the first time she had spoken since she entered the hospital. She had not uttered a word for two weeks. She selected a dark blue paper and painted a snowy fir forest. She was quite capable. It was beautiful. Later when they hung it up in the living room of the hospital, all the patients gathered around admiring this beautiful painting, and that broke her withdrawal.

One of the most frequent reactions to this project, especially in the highly disturbed patient, is one of wanting direction. "If you do it first and show me, then I am willing to do it. If I'm left on my own I'll fumble, but if I get firm direction, I am willing to work." That sounds contradictory because if one assumes that the psychotic is not cooperating with common sense or with common thinking, then the reaction would be rebellion. However, this reminds me of something I've heard Dreikurs say, that with psychotic children you don't give choices. You give them directions and you're firm in your direction, because you need to get them into some kind of movement.

Follow-up Sessions

I have said that the assigned paintings are a test, and it's important that there are several subsequent sessions after this to follow up on problems and work out the situation. For instance, in the case of two or three participants who are still rebellious, I try to work this out in discussion. "What is it that you're saying when you don't follow instructions? What's going on in your mind?" Or I might guess at the hidden reason, "May I guess what is happening?" I try to win them over through discussion and guessing the hidden reason behind the rebellion.

I might turn to the group instead, and ask them if they can guess why John, for example, refuses and feels it's so difficult to follow instructions. By then we may have had so many discussions that they can make guesses and often hit upon the hidden reason themselves. The guesses may be very primitive or very sophisticated, depending on the group and their observations.

Determining the Final Session

The results of this activity help me in planning the last two or three sessions. If participants have experienced pleasure in having an assignment and painting something realistic, it would indicate to me a desire to deal with the real world and to know exactly where they are—whether their feet are solidly rooted in the ground or still floating in mid-air. Then perhaps the next assignment would be to paint a city together as a group, or I might give them all a group assignment with a special topic to satisfy this desire for realism. As a group they would help each other with the necessary skills. I first developed this idea of group painting with juvenile delinquents. The people who are more capable of realistically portraying subject matter do that part of it and carry along those who have not yet developed this ability, so that through this cooperative effort the end product is one that is satisfying to the whole group.

If I discover that the majority of the group have not been able to carry out the assignment realistically and are still fumbling and struggling with the idea that "it has to be recognizable or I have not fulfilled my assignment," we might go back to the carousel activity, with the instructions that "Now this time, start out with something very real that you want to complete, and then when I say change, move to the next place, and try to complete what you think that person had intended to express, so that the end result will be a group of paintings that are representational and recognizable rather than abstract."

PAINTING A GIFT

As a general rule, either at the last group session or near the end of a workshop, I suggest that the participants tell their neighbors to the right what they would like to have painted for them as a farewell present to remember the experience which they have shared. This usually produces a great feeling of closeness and pleasure. After they have painted what their partner has requested, the results are displayed, and I ask, "Did you get what you asked for? Are you pleased with it?" Then we discuss what the project means to each one.

Ability to Give and Receive

Fundamentally, my rationale for this project is what I remember Dreikurs (1969) saying to depressed patients: "Do one thing a day for another person and you will begin to feel that you have some reason for living." Painting something for another person can be the first step for a depressed patient.

There are many people who are so proud that, while it is easy for them to give something, it is very difficult for them to receive service. This activity presents a challenge for them. They have an experience in receiving something graciously as well as contributing something to somebody else's pleasure as a memory.

For the person who has been independent and in a leadership role throughout life, the mere shock of suddenly being left in a subordinate position, as with a stroke or because of depression or losing a job, can mean that, "Now I am thoroughly worthless because I sit here helplessly and people serve me and I can't do anything to serve them. I want to do the serving and I don't want to receive." Therefore, in the course of the discussion that follows after this project, each person is asked, "What is your reaction when you get a present? How do you feel about it? How do you feel about giving something to someone?" Then, of course, we uncover a variety of reactions to giving and receiving.

An Example

I have a story that a friend of mine in Israel told about her aged father who until his eighties was the chief person in the community. He acted as counselor or advisor for everyone. All his life he was in a position to guide and to do things for his community, for his immediate family, and for all concerned. Suddenly he had a stroke. When his daughter came to visit him he said to her, "Would you be kind enough to go to the pharmacist's and see if you can get some medication so that I can put myself to death, because it is impossible for me to live now that I am useless and everybody has to wait on me. I no longer want to live." Her response to him was, "Father, you don't know what you are saying. Do you not realize what an important contribution you are now making to our lives? Never in your life have we been able to do anything for you, and now we are in a position to show you how much we care for you, and it ennobles our lives. It is a privilege for my children to be able to serve their grandfather. You are not useless. You serve as a wonderful example to us of being able now to sit back and permit us to do things for you, so please go on living."*

The Need to Please

This exercise in painting a gift for another produces some anxiety for the people who have as their basic mistake** the conviction that "unless I can please I am nothing" (Dreikurs, 1972). Since they are now put in a position of having to please, and because of the lack of skill in executing what the other person has requested, they may be afraid of producing something that will give displeasure.

The usual response to asking "Were you pleased by what you received," is "Yes, I like it so much, and I'm going to keep it forever. What a great pleasure! You did it just for me, and this is such a good memory of our experience together. I'll remember it for the rest of my life because I'm going to hang it up in my room and look at it. You did it for me and you pleased me." In the case of not pleasing, the question might be, "It is possible that you were afraid your painting would not please the other person?"

---

*Gemeinschaftsgefuhl explicated means that being a part of the human community requires allowing others to give to you and not just you doing the giving. In the cultures where there are social stratifications which denote some as superior and some as inferior and all people are ranked according to their worth, the strong (superior) always reach "down" to help those regarded as inferior. A democracy declares equality, and won't function properly if some members set themselves above the group by refusing to accept offerings from others (Dreikurs, 1972).

**Adler (1969) proposed the idea that all neurotic and psychotic behavior is characterized by flaws in logic. These flaws are referred to as "basic mistakes." These mistakes are usually not in the individual's awareness and were probably more appropriate in childhood. Individuals develop in a unique environment from all other individuals. As developing children attempt to make sense of their environment and their place in that environment, they are bound to draw conclusions, based upon their unique situation, which are not applicable to the wider community. When these mistaken conclusions, basic mistakes, interfere with interpersonal relationships to a pathological degree, they become synonymous with Horney's "overdriven attitude" (Hall and Lindzey, 1957). They are basic mistakes about one's self, other people and the environment and are irrational, impossible, inappropriate, intolerant, . . . egocentric, vindictive, compulsive, and insatiable (Shulman, 1973).

The Perfectionist

However, a participant will occasionally say, "I don't like what you did. I don't want to remember it." Then we talk about this. I might ask, "What are you thinking about? What would you have preferred it to be? What is it about the painting that you don't like?" A variety of biased apperceptions surface in such a discussion, the most frequent being that the perfectionist is never pleased with anything (Dreikurs, 1972). "It isn't perfect enough. Therefore I'm displeased. I wanted it to be exactly the way I had visualized it, and since it isn't perfect, I don't accept it, I don't like it." We then talk about the perfectionistic lifestyle.

In order to draw out the hidden reason of the perfectionist, I will venture a guess such as "Would you permit me to guess why you are displeased? I may be wrong, and perhaps the guess has nothing to do with what you are thinking, but it is possible that unless it is the perfect production you expected, you don't like it?" Usually that elicits a smile of recognition. "Yes, that's exactly right. I like things to be perfect." This guessing method dramatically exposes the basic mistakes in one's lifestyle. I don't assess the lifestyle,* but I touch on it when I probe for the hidden reason.**

Feelings Follow Thoughts

I also use the questions "What are you thinking at this moment, and how do you feel?" as a demonstration of "I am not the hopeless victim of my emotions. I think something and then produce the emotion to codify my thoughts." For example, when I ask the participants at the end of the session what

---

*Adler (1964) defined Life Style as the "Unique Law of Movement" of any individual. Life Style is the term that Adlerians would use in place of "personality." Adler sees all drives, strivings, tendencies and aspirations as a part of a unified gestalt which was at all times directed by the individual's unique law of movement (Shulman, 1973).

**Dreikurs (Shulman, 1973) developed the concept of "hidden reason" to explain the immediate motivation of the individual in a given situation. It is the individual's unique justification for a specific behavior – i.e., the adolescent girl is accused of lying to her parents about her whereabouts on the previous evening; therefore, she says to herself (the hidden reason), "Since they don't trust me anyway, I may as well go out now and lie as to my intentions." The hidden reason generates feelings to support the thoughts which one has just created. It is the rationalization which people produce to make their immediate behavior acceptable to themselves.

each one learned from the experience, someone will say something like, "I learned a great deal," and I will then respond, "What are you thinking about right now?"

"I'm thinking what fun it was to be here."

"And how do you feel?" "I feel happy. It was fun, so I'm happy." That is a positive reaction, and I use it as a potent demonstration of how we generate feelings to correspond with our thoughts.

When someone makes a comment that is ripe for probing (now what does that statement really mean), then I follow this gold mine.* I use the gold mine and the hidden reason in all of my work, and for these, of course, I am grateful to Rudolf Dreikurs. I explain these mechanisms in a simple way, without going into theoretical, intellectual polemics. Thinking "It was fun to be here, and therefore I'm happy" is a very simple explanation of how thinking and feeling are related.

---

*By "gold mine" I mean that I have discovered a cue to the hidden reason. The cue to the gold mine is a qualifying word by the individual. The most common of these is "but." Seemingly irrational behavior or statements following a suggestion to the individual are followed by "yes, but." For example, saying to the person, "Wouldn't it be reasonable if you walked away from your husband knowing that he was going to hit you?" Then comes the reply: "Yes, but if I walked away he would then go get drunk and get thrown in jail."

"Gold mine" and "hidden reason" are really synonymous. Another common cue that lets me know when I've hit upon a gold mine is the hospitalized patient's initial statement to me. "I don't know what I'm doing here anyway."

More on General Methods

Sequence Flexibility

Most art therapy sessions last from one and a half to three hours, including the group cooperation time involved in preparation of materials, painting, and discussion. My usual procedure is to start a new group with a semi-structured activity and then in subsequent sessions move to a more structured one, a loosely structured one, and then to a completely unstructured project, continuing in this manner unless a need arises to vary the sequence.

However, it is of utmost importance for me to be completely flexible. Although I have an idea what I'd like to do with a group on any particular day, I see it as my job to respond to the needs of the immediate situation, to fit into the mood of the group, and to follow up on comments from participants – to dig the gold mine,* so to speak.

Digging the Gold Mine

I follow closely Dreikurs' admonition, "If you hear something, react at the moment because you're liable to forget it." When someone in the group says something which lends itself to further exploration or a different kind of project, I don't put it off. The freshness could be lost and the response of the group diminished if I were to delay or make a note to do it another time.

This reminds me of Andre L'Hote's first instruction to us as painters: "Put down on paper your immediate spontaneous reaction to the subject. Don't wait to do it later. That first fresh response is the most potent to work with because your creativity is at its height."

---

*"Gold mine" is a term coined by Rudolf Dreikurs which refers to an especially fruitful expression by the patient. The therapist is constantly alert to such expressions as they pinpoint key issues for the patient. "Digging the gold mine" means following up on these expressions: mining the precious material.

Comments from participants have often inspired me to deviate from my usual routine, and occasionally these changes have resulted in a successful new project which I've since incorporated into my regular sequence—for example, "Paint as a child."

A Mood Changing Process

An art therapy session sometimes becomes a mood changing process, and I can facilitate this most effectively by first assessing and fitting in with the atmosphere of the group. This permits me to lead the group into another, perhaps more constructive mood, through the use of specific projects designed to work with the immediate needs of the group. Destructive hyperactive teenagers may respond best to the tearing paper exercise, for example. Depressed patients, those who enter in a very high, elated spirit, or a group which is quite anxious will all need different kinds of activities related to their present mood.

Art therapy is, then, a creative process for the therapist, as well as the participants, and, although I could present here a specific outline for conducting an art therapy sequence, readers would probably be better off keeping my framework and projects in mind but innovating as they find gold mines of their own and being responsive to the immediate group situation in which they find themselves.

Modification of Basic Framework

It would be reasonable to say that the framework I have developed for working with groups could be modified for use with individuals, groups of couples, families, geriatric groups, and in industry. The way this is done would depend on the therapist's creativity, spontaneity, knowledge of Individual Psychology, experience in art and with its materials, and the rapport which can be established with the group. I vary the introduction only slightly according to the group of people involved.

Although groups enable me to develop social interest in participants, enhancing this simply because of the dynamics involved in a group, the use of a group is not a requisite for art therapy. I have not worked with individuals myself, but

114

others have done this successfully, and as long as a relationship is developed with even one other person, therapy can occur.

Working with Professionals

Whereas groups of hospital patients in art therapy are open-ended and ongoing, professionals are usually taking art therapy as a class, workshop, or in some special setting with time limits. At the Alfred Adler Institute in Chicago I pace my time to correspond with semester requirements which are 22 hours. It is sometimes possible to set aside two or three weekends or to work for five hours on four consecutive Saturdays, which allows for enough time for professionals to experience the process as participants.

Art Therapy as an Adjunct to Group Therapy

Although I'm not aware of any such arrangement currently in existence, I've suggested that art therapy might be a very effective way to start a new group. Using the carousel activity as a warming up exercise to help members get to know each other could facilitate group cohesiveness. Painting together on the same piece of paper without speaking, in either pairs or small groups, is another project which would be a good preparation for group psychotherapy, particularly for a fairly new group whose members are not yet well acquainted.

I can envision art therapy sessions being interspersed with group therapy at regular intervals, so that nonverbal experience can reinforce what is worked on verbally at other times. For example, an individual's movement in life, which is revealed in an early recollection, is the same whether it is painted or given verbally, and the impact of this information is more powerful when both methods are experienced. In fact, one might also incorporate art therapy with action therapy, music therapy or psychodrama, creating an all-inclusive experience.

Follow-Up with Patients Who Need More Help

People have asked me if art therapy participants have ever had a break with reality or some other abreaction during a session, but in fact my experience is the reverse. There is usually a reduction in psychotic behavior. The general mood at the close of each session is one of complete relaxation and sometimes even exhilaration.

However, I am concerned that the experience may be a very traumatic one for some people, and there is always a chance that the information revealed during a session might be a shock to someone. This is particularly true for the carousel activity because it is the first project and I may not be well acquainted with participants. I therefore preface my remarks before the discussion following the carousel activity with, "If anything is said which hurts you or in any way affects you, and you can't talk about it now, please be sure to talk to me, or a friend or therapist later."

In addition, I observe carefully how each one responds to what is said during the discussion, and if I sense that something is wrong or that someone is upset, I will ask before that person leaves, "Do you want to talk to me or is there someone else you'd like to talk with about this? Let's not leave it up in the air." If the person has a therapist I will make a call to ensure a follow-up contact.

Another strategy I use to check out how participants are reacting to the process is to ask at the opening of each session, "What do you recall from last time; what was outstanding about the last session?" I learned this from Dr. Dreikurs. Often a person who was distressed by our previous meeting will bring it up at this time. It is the most potent learning experience which is remembered.

I usually proceed with the assumption that people are not too fragile and that they can tolerate whatever may be discussed when we're together. Although it's always a potential danger, I've never heard of anyone who has been adversely affected as a result of an experience in art therapy.

Group Composition

ART THERAPY WITH HOSPITALIZED PATIENTS

I first began using art therapy, as I now conceive of it, in 1962 with Dr. Bernard Shulman's patients at St. Joseph Hospital. Working in a hospital poses a different problem than working with "normal" people. However, the similarities are striking, and I'd like to explain how I came to this conclusion and why I was encouraged to step out of the hospital situation, work with non-psychotic groups and teach my methods to others at various Adlerian institutes.

After about three or four months in the hospital, the head nurse said to me, "What do you do with the patients? After a session many of them come out in an entirely different mood. They are relaxed and sometimes there is even an improvement in some of the very severe cases. They begin to have more reality in their conversation and less withdrawal. What do you do?" My response was, "It's very difficult for me to describe verbally a nonverbal experience. Will you and your staff come in and share the experience and pretend you're patients and let me work with you in the same manner?"

Working with the Staff

As they came in the door I proceeded to greet them as I would greet patients, but these strong leaders could not pretend. I greeted the first one at the door saying, "Hello, my name is Tee. You may call me Tee." I saw this grin on her face, and I continued, "What's your name?" She said, "Oh, come off it, you know I'm Beth!" Another said, "I've been here three years, you know me." "Okay, let's forget the shenanigans about pretending you're patients. Just come in."

We went ahead with the carousel activity and then put all the paintings on the wall. I asked only "which one do you like and why do you like it?"

Similarities with Staff

After I had spoken to two or three, the head nurse said, "My goodness, Tee, what we did resembles exactly what the patients did. Are we crazy too?" I said, "Margaret, just the opposite is true. When the patients are in here, they are not crazy. They are working on a project. They are concentrating on a task. I treat them as if they were not patients in the hospital, and what they produce is the same as yours because at least for the time being they are not crazy. They are working together as a group. They are treated as healthy human beings. They are experiencing an approach, an atmosphere that they do not experience on the unit, because there's no medication, there's no nurse's uniform, there are no doctors coming around in the workroom where we're doing the job. There are times when you who are sophisticated will recognize certain tendencies that indicate agitation and distress. However, I can see that in your group, too, because not all of you are at peace with yourselves. All of you have certain idiosyncracies, and they come out when you are painting. You can't escape it, any more than you can escape your handwriting. It is a rhythm that you have, and you'll follow it in any situation."

This experience gave me courage to work with other groups of people, because the staff in this project were not just participants learning a new technique or new method, but were experiencing self-awareness and learning how they functioned under certain circumstances.

It may seem peculiar that I needed encouragement to work with people who were not psychotic. It soon became clear to me, after beginning art therapy with hospital patients, that one can work effectively with a psychotic patient if one is not afraid of the unanticipated and is willing to make a mistake and just experiment.

The Appeal of Art Therapy

While I was working only with Dr. Shulman's patients, the art work was displayed in the general sitting room. The other patients came around and frequently made remarks such as "This is kids' stuff," but the patients who were involved with the art therapy took it upon themselves to be mini art educators and to introduce to the other patients what was happening.

In a short time the others came to the door of our room and wanted access. At this time we didn't have enough space, and we also didn't have the approval of the other psychiatrists. Dr. Shulman was able to obtain this permission, we opened up the sessions to everyone, and we moved to a large room used for occupational therapy on another floor.

This provided the patients with an open environment, out of their locked ward, in a room where many people did things with their hands. The difference in working with them here was remarkable. They became more open and free away from their ward and as I paid less attention to what was going on, which I was doing out of necessity since the group was so large.

No Observers

This experience gave me the idea that observation is not helpful, and since then my rule has been "We have no observers." If people wish to see what my groups are doing, they come as participants and are part of the group.

Less observation produces more, and people feel freer to express themselves because no one is standing by evaluating what they're doing. Having no observers served another purpose. When visitors came, not knowing any skills, the patients were able to help them. They could see that they were really quite competent, that they knew what to do, whereas the outsiders, the "normal" ones, were clumsy and didn't know what to do. It was encouraging for the patients.

Breaking through Psychosis

The carousel affords a marvelous opportunity to break through a patient's psychosis. There are some psychotics who have completely enclosed themselves in glass cages which no one can penetrate and within which they can be supreme, all powerful, and avoid common sense thinking as well as relationships with others which are painful (Dreikurs, 1956). There are others, however, who do communicate and who function quite adequately in certain areas of their lives.

When I introduce the carousel project, the psychotic who is completely withdrawn usually doesn't respond at all, and just sits. I ask the usual questions such as, "Why do you think we have music, and why do I ask you to choose your own paper?" but there is no way of knowing how much this person understands or has awareness. Sometimes a patient will tell me later exactly what went on.

The Influence of the Group

When faced with a piece of paper and everyone else is dipping into the paint and listening to music, even withdrawn patients are usually willing to participate. The group rhythm and nonverbal group pressure are enough to get them going. With the blank piece of paper, patients are in business for themselves and need not conform to anyone else's rhythm or pattern of thinking. They happily paint a dot, a stroke, or just a blob, or even elect to upset a jar of paint on the paper.

A curious thing happens when the severely psychotic patients are asked to change positions in the carousel and paint on what someone else has started. After the first change there is usually a lot of room left on the paper, and they can still be on their own. After the next change the paper begins to be more filled. By the time they get to the fifth paper they are thoroughly frustrated because they either have to follow the rhythm already begun or do something else. They have to decide what to do. They could become violent or walk out or destroy the paper, but this has never happened. They could take a new piece of paper and go off alone to paint, but so far that has not happened either. They often take another brush, preferably a very large one, dip it into either black or dark blue paint, and obliterate everything that went before. I say "change" again, and they proceed to obliterate the next one.

Those who are not as deeply into a psychosis and have already experienced the fun of producing something may rescue the destruction as they follow behind it. They may dribble white paint on it so that it becomes a sky of stars or put some yellow spots on it so it becomes a field of daisies.

The Futility of Destruction

By this time, the severely psychotic patients have obliterated four or five paintings and are frustrated again, because the destruction serves no purpose. I haven't told them to stop destroying, no one else has commented on it at all, and they are again faced with a decision to continue destroying, walk out, or start to paint. Almost invariably they begin to paint, although not necessarily following the rhythm already established. As soon as one finds a little empty space and begins to paint, the complete isolation has been penetrated, even if only slightly, like a pin-prick. This is the major advantage of the carousel project in working with patients in a psychiatric unit.

Painting on the Same Paper

The next project I use with patients is usually the one in which two people paint on the same piece of paper; however, I don't necessarily ask them to do it without speaking to each other, and the rationale for the project is different than when working with a non-psychotic population. For the latter I want to demonstrate how family constellation factors apply to the movement expressed by participants when they have to paint together without communicating. In the hospital I choose the partners who will work together on the basis of their rhythm and personality characteristics. For example, I might ask someone who seems to be very tense and perfectionistic to work with someone who is quite slovenly. "Are you willing to work together? One can start and the other one follow." This enables people to change their rhythm. One influences the other.

I recall a religious woman in the psychiatric unit who was really quite disturbed. She left about a three-inch space at the bottom of the paper on everything she painted. I suggested, "Sally, would you be willing to turn the paper around, because what you are now doing indicates that you're up in the air thinking of your life beyond and you're not down to earth. See if you can fill in the space and bring yourself down to earth."

Open Ended Session

Art therapy with hospitalized psychiatric patients tends to be an ongoing program, some people coming for two or three sessions and some continuing for three or four months or more, depending on residence limitations. The new members of the group are encouraged by the others who share with me the responsibility of easing newcomers into the situation, without any solicitation from me. The process of working and painting together as a group evokes considerable caring and concern for each other. There's a great tenderness shown to new people,

121

especially if the patient is quite agitated, upset, or apprehensive about the new experience. One, two, or three patients will take new persons under their wings, so to speak, and guide them. They take over, which, of course, is good for them as well as helpful for me.

The Development of Caring

This caring for each other and feeling of belonging is perhaps the most therapeutic outcome of the group approach. As soon as a close-knit relationship develops from working on the same project, there is a strong feeling of caring for each other and being proud when somebody accomplishes something. In a short time patients become very devoted and attached to each other. For instance, there have been incidents when a patient who has participated very little suddenly paints something and it is put up on the wall, and the rest of the group spontaneously applauds, "That's great! We like what you did so well." No matter what a newcomer does, they usually encourage by saying, "Oh, that's nice" or something of that sort. I don't encourage applause or compliments, but these are spontaneous reactions and are quite an experience for someone who has not had any encouragement for a long time, if ever.

I remember a rather elderly woman who was in a senile psychosis. We were doing the changing carousel activity. There was a young man next to her, and she just didn't know what to do. He kept whispering in her ear what to do next. She had started her painting with just a circle, and by the time it came around to her again, the others had changed it into quite a wonderful clown. This clown had on a checked blouse, and she didn't know what to do with it. He whispered in her ear, "Put red buttons on it." Then when they put it on the wall she ran to it with pride and said, "I finished it, and I made it beautiful with my red buttons."

Deferring Leadership

There are times when I let the group take over leadership of the painting session. I have done this on occasions when there are a number of new patients entering the ongoing art therapy program. The more experienced members of the group then decide how they will conduct the session. Usually several people will take on various responsibilities, for deciding which

122

art activity to use, conducting the discussion, putting up the paintings, etc. My role then becomes a participant in the activity. I'm a member of the group.

Cases

The following cases illustrate some of the methods I've developed for use with psychotic patients. Names and circumstances have been changed so as to protect the identity of the patients, but the process and examples are in keeping and fit the principles which I am illustrating.

Sharon.

One day a very obese new patient walked in carrying a shopping bag and basket. She sat down, put her bag on another chair and the basket on still another. Since I needed those two spaces I approached her, asking, "Would you mind putting your things underneath or on the side?"

"I very much would mind. I want these things with me."

I let it go at that and walked away, but as soon as I started to explain the project she interrupted, "Madame, what you're doing here is a bunch of nonsense. You don't know what you are doing. You will never know what I know about art. *I* am a graduate of the Art Institute, and *I* can tell you much, much more about art than you will ever know."

I addressed her by name and said, "I would be very pleased to learn from you. Would you like to take over the session and I'll take your place, and you conduct what we're doing?"

She said, "No, I don't want to do that."

"All right, I'll proceed."

After I had talked about what we were going to do and had put on the music she said to me, "I don't want to paint, but I would really love to dance. I haven't danced for years."

Even though this is not my routine, I said, "Please dance." She then took the bag and basket off the two chairs and proceeded to dance to the music all through the period. Not one other patient turned around to look at her during the activity. Before we started the discussion, she asked to go back to her unit in the hospital, and I had her escorted back.

Later when we were discussing the painting activity I remarked on the fact that Sharon had been dancing and no one had seemed to notice. The others said, "We wouldn't give her the satisfaction of looking at her. She walks around the unit as if she were the queen, and acts as if she knows better than anyone." To my amazement at the next session Sharon came to me and said, "If you really would like me to help, I would like to work with you." She became a great help to me, especially when elderly people joined the group who were not willing to paint anything except a realistic object. They might say, "I'd like to learn to paint that flower," and I would ask Sharon to instruct them. I used her to teach participants to paint.*

She became one of the most constructive helpers on the unit after that, because she changed from the person who acted superior to a helper who really wanted to be part of the group. Refusing to enter into a power struggle with her and giving her permission to do what she wanted minimized her psychosis and turned her destructive behavior into constructive action. The nurses reported that after this experience she contributed much more on the unit.

Another woman with a large basket came into the art therapy room one day when I was working with a small group. When I tried to communicate with her she said, "No speak English. Speak Polish." She proceeded to gather everything off the table and put it in her basket, and when I said, "Would you like to join us and paint?" she said something in Polish which was probably derogatory.

Another participant who spoke Polish started quarreling with her, telling her to be quiet. While this fight was going on I thought, "Why is she gathering up everything from the table? What does that movement mean? Perhaps she feels deprived and this is her way of getting."

I had just finished a painting and I said to her, "Elizabeth, would you like me to give you this painting?" "Yes," she answered, and grabbed it from me. She had understood me perfectly. My next statement was, "You'd better take it to your room immediately or someone will take it away from you."

When she left the room I locked the door before the two of them could resume their fighting. This maneuver didn't particularly help Elizabeth, but guessing what her movement was

---

*Adler pointed out that if one has not learned that the purpose of life is to serve others, they have missed the point of living. Emotional health means serving others (Adler, 1931).

and the meaning of her behavior allowed me to deal with a potentially violent outbreak and to continue the group activity without serious interruption.

Crisis situations.

The training I received from Rudolf Dreikurs has been very helpful to me in crisis situations like this. On one occasion I was leaving the room after the patients had gone, and a very large woman came toward me down the corridor with her hands raised. I was sure she was going to strike me, and I was so petrified that I forgot Dreikurs' rule that showing fear will produce what is feared. I did remember another of his teachings, however, and I said, "You're much younger and stronger than I, and you can hurt me if you want to, and there isn't anything I can do about it" (Dreikurs, 1944). With that she walked away.

The unexpected.

Once a patient took a brush and bottle of paint and sipped the brush as if she were sipping from a straw. I asked, "Does it taste good?" "Yes, it tastes good." I was afraid she'd start drinking the paint next, so I gave her some water and said, "Try this. It's a different flavor. She then proceeded to sip the water.

As with Elizabeth, the exchange did not help her, but a potentially dangerous situation was avoided. I refused to enter into a power struggle with the patient but at the same time was able to substitute a harmless substance for the paint.

A case of stuttering.

Alan was a young man whose stuttering problem was so severe that he had became violent and had to be hospitalized. He was sent to art therapy on his first day out of restraint. He wouldn't paint, and he didn't speak at all because it was torture for him. He removed himself from the group and and drew instead. When I looked at what he had drawn I was truly amazed, for it was magnificent, as if he had trained with an old master.

I said, "Alan, don't answer me. Just nod your head. Have you ever studied drawing?" He shook his head no. "Did you learn it on your own?" He nodded yes. "It seems, Alan, if you don't *have* to do something you do it well."

When we were talking about the paintings later and it was Alan's turn, I had an idea. I walked up to him and said, "Alan,

I'm sorry I'm not 50 years younger. We would make a wonderful pair of lovers. You see, my hearing aid isn't working and I can hardly hear what's going on. Now if we were lovers, you wouldn't have to speak because I couldn't hear you."

He answered, "And then we'd be an odd couple" without stuttering. From then on for the rest of his time in the hospital, when he spoke to me he didn't stutter at all. He continued to stutter otherwise, but it was diminished through medication and therapy. One day when I was leaving the hospital after a group session he came to me and whispered in my ear, "Let's get married anyhow, Love. We would be a wonderful couple."

Beth and Catherine.

This case is a good example of what happens when patients begin to care for each other. One day a middle-aged person came into the room after we had already started. She saw the name Dreikurs on my name tag and proceeded to have a fit of hysteria. She cried, "Oh, Dreikurs! Ten years ago I had therapy with him and he helped me so much. Now he's gone and no one can help me. I'm lost."

I wanted to take her in my arms and cry with her, so I said, "Beth, I want to cry too, but I haven't the time. I have a job to do. Would you be kind enough to sit down and cry for both of us?" She did this and had a good cry.

One of the other participants, a tender, overprotective person by the name of Catherine, said, "Beth, please don't cry. You'll break my heart." My response was, "Catherine, Beth has the right to cry if she wishes. I don't think we should ask her to stop if she wants to cry. However, if it bothers you or anyone else, I will ask her to leave the room until she's through crying."

"No, no, we want her to stay," was the answer, and Catherine walked out of the room, went to the nursing station, and brought back an ice bag, put it on Beth's head, and said, "This will make you feel better."

The sobbing was somewhat reduced, but I decided to change the art project to the tearing and pasting paper activity because of her agitation. Everyone was happy pasting except Beth, who crumbled the torn paper into bits. Catherine then sat down next to her and each time straightened out the bit of paper, put paste on it, took Beth's hand and said, "Paste it on here, Beth."

When we were ready to display the results, Beth's collage was greatly admired and she was much calmer. I asked the patients, "Is there something you learned today that's helpful, or have you changed in any way?" Beth said, "I feel relaxed and I know I'm going to get well."

"How do you know that?"

"Because I feel how warm and kind people are. It isn't only Dr. Dreikurs who can help me. Other people can help me, too, so I know I'm going to get well."

Another motive.

Beth went on to say, "The most important thing I learned today is that I don't have to be afraid of my daughter. My daughter is a fine painter. I have always wanted to paint but I never dared because I thought she wouldn't like it. Now I don't care if she likes it or not, I'm going to become a painter too." This was the beginning of Beth's improvement, and indeed she was only in the hospital for a week after that.

I Have No Name.

Another time during a painting session a woman came in, again with a huge basket and valise, wearing a straw hat with a plume. Her lips were painted black and her face many hues, haphazardly applied. She walked up to me, and I greeted her, "Hello, my name is Tee. What's yours?"

"I have no name."

"I Have No Name, would you like to paint?"

"Sh —."

"I Have No Name, please paint sh —." She took a brush and painted sh —.

"I Have No Name, that's pretty sh —. Paint more." She pretended to intensify the color and looked up at me wondering what I was going to say next.

"I Have No Name, do you think you can paint something other than sh —?"

"Sh —."

"I Have No Name, would you like a new paper?" She took another paper and sat down. I wasn't sure whether or not she would be destructive. There was an empty place next to her, so I sat beside her with a blank paper and proceeded to paint. She sat there mumbling gibberish. I repeated every word she said, prefacing it with "I Have No Name" each time.

After awhile I said, "I Have No Name, I don't want to talk to you anymore. I want to work. If you want to work, go ahead." She did. She painted quite a bizzare scene, left the room, and came back again in time to look at the paintings.

The patients, who were nearly as disturbed as she, loved her painting. They seemed to understand it and praised what she did very highly.

At the end, she was the only one who hadn't had a chance to speak. I said, "I Have No Name, you may choose what you like and tell us about it." She turned around and said, "Tee, my name is Ruth." This was the first breakthrough in her psychotic state, and she continued to talk on a more rational level with others.

PAINTING WITH FAMILIES AND COUPLES

I've been asked by participants, "Do you think I could use these painting activities with my family as recreation?" Of course the answer is yes. The activities themselves are interesting projects for all family members to work on together. A family may find the experience so satisfying and enjoyable that they want to pursue it with other families in a recreational setting or to beautify the home or neighborhood. "What can we do about improving the way our house looks by working together as a family or as a group of families? How can we utilize our efforts for the benefit of all?"

Aside from family recreational use of the painting projects I've described, they can be quite enlightening when expanded for use with several families who are in family therapy or with family study groups, often associated with Adlerian family education centers. In one instance, three families were gathered together at a college in Israel. The initial activity was the carousel. The parents were asked to paint with the children of another family first, and then with their own children. The parents and children then painted in two separate groups, followed by the whole group painting together.

Discussion with Families

Discussion which ensues after family painting activities center on, "What is the difference when you paint with your own children, and what is the difference for the children when

128

they paint with their parents, as opposed to others?" This usually results in the parents recognizing the extent to which they are still dominating and controlling their children's lives, in spite of the fact that they are members of a study group and are practicing to relinquish control, domination, and ownership of their children. The children often experience that they are more willing to work with other children's parents than their own, because they feel they have nothing to rebel against. These are just other people. However, the rebellious child will sometimes rebel against any adult.

It's also not true that all the children paint harmoniously together. The usual antagonisms crop up, especially when there are teenagers along with younger children. Superiority/inferiority feelings often surface, and competition among siblings is expressed, not just in the family but in the group. We can see whether they're able to cooperate no matter what their age, or whether there's a feeling of, for example, "Oh, I am more than you because I'm fifteen and you're only a little squirt, you're only ten." That could come out, and would be open for discussion. This painting exercise lends itself to lengthy group discussions and exchange about what happens when we encounter a strange parent versus our own parent, what happens when we work with our own children or our neighbor's children. A new dimension is added to family therapy with the use of painting as a springboard by which many of the reactions and difficulties are brought to light and can be discussed.

Planning Projects

How art therapy is pursued with families varies with the size and nature of the group. The leader needs to sense when a group is ready to experiment with this kind of activity, and should work out a plan with the group using the projects which meet their needs.

After the carousel activity, with parents and children shifting places, and the initial discussion about what was experienced and the differences encountered, the families can be presented with various possibilities for other painting experiences. This is a good time for a family discussion in which all members are invited to participate. All are involved in planning and decision making.

Aside from the other painting activities previously described, there are other possibilities for shifting group members which also elicit valuable information for discussion. For example, the children can all work together as a group and the parents as another group. Many of the same dynamics occur as those encountered with any group of people who are beginning art therapy and who do not know each other. They begin to understand each other through their cooperation and shared responsibility. The goal, especially at first, is always to enhance social interest and encourage a sense of belonging.

Mixed Ages

Although some people may feel that it's difficult to work with families when the children are of mixed ages, I have not found this to be an insurmountable problem. As a matter of fact, I have had very young children fit easily into a group of adults in Israel when parents could not get babysitters and therefore brought their children to the group. Quite naturally one has to consider the physical setting so that two-year-olds can be part of the group with fifteen-year-olds. If it were not possible for a child to reach something, it may increase the sense of being an inferior member of the group because "I am not able to do it but the rest of them can."

Although the facilities may have to be reconstructed to allow for the differing sizes of all ages included, working with age differences per se would not be different from working with any mixed group of people. A few members will have achieved some facility with paints, having handled them before. Others have never touched paint and may be quite discouraged with the prospect. The carousel project is a good activity to use with mixed ages, especially if it's introduced with the idea that the purpose is not to produce a painting, but to see what will develop from a group effort and to enjoy the process.

It would be interesting to experiment with multi-generation families in art therapy. The leader would need to be very skilled in order to sense at what point to separate groups of grandparents, parents, and children, and when to mix them to see what new relationships can be formed by interchanging generations.

Painting with Couples

I'd work with couples in much the same way as families, having several couples interchange partners and work with each other, varying the sequence to see what happens to relationships under different circumstances. The direction taken in subsequent discussion will depend on the nature of the conflicts the couples are having. The procedure would be similar to my usual approach — to meet the people and the situation I have to work with, and then spontaneously and creatively devise the kind of project or sequence which will help me encourage participants to come to grips with their problems. In discussion I might ask, "How did you feel about painting together as husband and wife? What did you experience? What do you know about your mate that you didn't know before?"

One of the most illuminating projects for couples would be painting on the same piece of paper without talking to each other or signaling to each other, followed by the small individual painting (see chapter entitled Paint on the Same Paper). I'd ask in discussion, "What does this person tell you in the small painting? What is the reaction to what happened when two painted together, and what have you learned about each other?" Then I might go into family constellations and ask, "Why do you react to each other this way when painting?" I'd improvise according to the needs of the situation and the particular problems of the couples participating.

PAINTING WITH OLDER PERSONS

The use of art therapy with the elderly is a virgin field, certainly one which is ripe for experimentation and which is much needed. I would suggest approaching this group in much the same way as very young children, in the sense of moving slowly and encouraging them to relax and *be,* rather than being concerned about results. It might be difficult to accomplish this with older people, especially with a sophisticated group who may have rigid standards and find it hard to accept something less than perfection in their paintings, or who have learned to admire only that which is completely realistic. It involves changing established ideas about what is beautiful and what is not. I might say something like, "This is not a project in which you are learning to be a painter or are expected to produce anything. See if you can just relax and enjoy the activity. Even if you'd like to make a real apple, for instance, see if you can accept something that is abstract and not really an apple but could make you think of an apple."

Freeing Up the Group

A good way to begin might be to ask them to do the opposite of what they've been trained to do: "Please paint the worst possible thing that you can. See if you can really mess this paper up, see what a bad picture you can paint." This procedure may help those for whom everything must be correct. They may then be willing to forget reality and experiment.

It's also possible that good results would be attained with divided groups. In that way the participants who wish to experiment may, and those who react and say, "I really don't want to experiment but I'd love to learn how to paint a flower," for example, can have a painting lesson about how to paint a flower. After the need to learn how to do it is satisfied, the individual might then be willing to experiment with other painting activities. Learning the feel of the brush or pen, pencil or crayon, so that they can make it do what they want, can be a liberating experience if they can then experiment with messing something up with the knowledge that nothing very horrendous is going to result.

Realistic Painting

Teaching the group — or part of it — how to paint something can be done at any time in the sequence of sessions. Often older people want to paint a flower, or apple, or copy a pretty picture. I teach them by actually taking their hand and saying, "Now follow what you see and put it down, put it down as you see it," and I guide their hand. Or I might say, "Look at it and paint it the way you see it. In the beginning your hand will not do what you want it to, but if you try several times your hand will gradually respond."

I will give them a real flower as a model, or a real apple, if that is what they're painting. Sometimes I say, "Paint each other. Paint a portrait of what you see. It probably won't look anything like that person, but use that as a guide. See if you
132

can paint the eyes, nose, ears, hair. It doesn't matter if it looks like the person or not, but use the person as a guide."

I think it would be an interesting experience if people faced each other. My guess is that the final result would look much more like their own portrait than the person whom they're painting. That's usually what happens in portrait painting. You somehow represent yourself rather than what you see. On the first page of Merjekovsky's book about Leonardo daVinci reproductions there is a self-portrait of the artist. It's my opinion that the Mona Lisa is just a female version of Leonardo daVinci.

Carousel

The carousel is probably the best of the projects I've described, for this group to begin with after the initial discomfort has dissipated. I say, "Start painting, and after awhile if you're willing to experiment and try something, I'll say 'change.' Then move to your right and paint on what you find in front of you." The next activity would be painting individually again, but not to paint the worst one. "Now paint one of your own."

Discussions with Older People

I'm very careful in my questioning of older people during the discussion period, because it could be a threatening situation for them. The reaction might be, "Oh, we don't want to come here. We don't want to be psychoanalyzed." I'd step gingerly in any psychological discussion until I got to know the group and could sense how comfortable they felt with each other and how willing they'd be to share. At first I'd merely ask them to put all the paintings, all three sets, on the wall and ask each person to pick out one they liked, and tell why they liked it and which part was especially pleasing. I'd ask the people to hang them in any way they wanted. "Do not be selective. Hang them all." If they only hang the so-called pretty ones and leave the others on the floor, it would be necessary to move into action and say, "Please remember, we're supposed to hang all the paintings. Now let's hang the rest of them, okay?" And they're likely then to pick out the worst efforts last and hang them all together. It might take several sessions before I'd have them select three they like and ask the group what the selections tell about the person. I would ask them if they would like to experience something a little different. "We all have very different tastes, and these tastes tell us something about us as human beings, what our preferences are."

Modifying the Discussion

With a group of older people I would recommend not asking what they do *not* like. If someone picked out a painting and said, "I hate that," this could be quite offensive to the person who painted it and could even discourage that person from proceeding and wanting to try again. I would stay on the positive side. "I like this and this is why I like it" rather than "I don't like it." It's every easy to discourage older persons who are set in their tastes and values and who have pet notions about what is good and bad, what is beautiful or disagreeable. If someone points to a painting and says, "I don't like it, it doesn't look like a cat," it can ruin the possibility of bringing that person in again, because of being criticized. The skill in working with older people is the essence of the skill of all therapists, to be creative and imaginative, to sense what's going on and to win them over with understanding. The art of all therapy is encouragement.* If participants feel encouraged they will cooperate with the leader's direction and choice of projects.

After the initial warming up using the carousel and the individual painting I may ask, "Do you think you would have been able to paint the one of your own if you hadn't had the experience of painting the worst possible one first and then sharing a painting activity with the group? Do you think it influenced you in any way? Did you feel more courageous in trying, or were you still timid?"

The Following Sessions

I might start the second session with "What was interesting to you about the carousel activity that we did the last time?" I would pick up what was interesting and go on from there. If the majority of the group said, "I liked it better when I painted my own picture," I might then do a session in which

---

*"Encouragement" is a term in Adlerian theory which is applied to a variety of situations. The term implies that the individuals who receive encouragement feel better about themselves, the situation or others (Dreikurs and Dinkmeyer, 1963).

everyone paints their own, and then the next session I .might ask, "Are you willing to try changing again?" Now this time when you change, paint something that you have in your mind, and see if the next person is willing to continue what you started." Much would depend on the atmosphere of the group, and how courageous the leader feels about giving choices and venturing into new areas.

WORKING WITH CHILDREN

The carousel and tearing paper exercises are two of the activities which work well with children, although other activities may also be appropriate depending on the age and experience of the group. The carousel is particularly helpful in the formation of groups. Children enjoy enormously the combination of action: painting and pasting a collage, which is involved in the tearing paper activity.

It is interesting to observe how the children function when they are given a free hand in the latter case. Do they exercise a certain restraint and keep the destruction in some kind of order, or do they go out of bounds and become destructive? Teenagers especially might turn this into a wild physical game. When the activity begins to get out of hand and it appears that it will become too destructive, I will say, "I think we'll stop for today and continue this another time." However, I don't hesitate to use this project with children because we are doing it for fun. "Let's play, let's tear it up and let's see what we can do with it."

I am very careful in preparing children for the carousel activity. The younger the child, the greater the need for preparation, and the more need for caution against the violation of their feeling of ownership. Children often feel, "This is mine and I do not want anyone to intrude. This is something very precious to me."

I change the sequence of the carousel for children out of respect for this feeling of ownership. I say something like, "First, paint a picture that is your very own, and put it aside and no one will touch it ... And now are you willing to see what comes out of our painting if we all share and paint on each other's?" It is very important to give them the opportunity of possession first. After both parts of the activity are completed, I may lead into a discussion by asking, "Which do you

135

prefer to do—paint by yourself or go around painting on each other's paper?"

The group leader is well advised not to question the children about what they are doing and why they're doing it; rather, "Would you like to tell us a story about the picture?" Instead of asking what the painting means in general, one could inquire about specific aspects of it. "The yellow in this is so beautiful. Even though I like the other colors too, I'm interested in what the yellow color in your picture means to you."

Discussion with children is quite effortless, and you can work out practically anything if you have the type of classroom that Dreikurs, Grunwald and Pepper suggest in their book, *Maintaining Sanity in the Classroom* (1971). The group will already have been introduced to the idea of discussing problems of individuals as well as group-related questions.

For projects like having two partners painting together or small group murals, the group can choose with whom they wish to work. This can be used as a sociogram, and can be very illuminating for the teacher without any written responses necessary. Asking "Whom would you like to work with" will show what the subgroups are in the classroom. Leaders may also want to give children a chance to choose one other person with whom they may share their own pictures.

When juvenile delinquents are involved in painting sessions, I can't visualize doing anything different from what I did when I first began using painting activities at Hull House, because the key is to shift the responsibility for the whole project to the destructive gang leader so that his leadership can be used constructively. I'd observe carefully, see who the leaders are, whether passive or active, and put them in charge of the situation so that they are responsible for what happens. Trying to draw them out in discussion or doing the carousel in order for them to become part of a group when there are others participating who are not delinquents just won't work.*

---

*Dreikurs (et al., 1959) referred to this method of working with the adolescents as "group leadership." The leader does not superimpose upon the group his or her ambitions, but provides group-centered guidance. This prevents the leader from coming into conflict with the gang leaders. Dreikurs advocates gaining the leader's cooperation by winning him or her over through enlisting the gang leader's strengths rather than attempting to challenge or compete with those strengths.

WORKING WITH GIRLS IN A REFORMATORY

In 1979, during one of my regular visits to Athens, Greece, I was asked to help with an unusual project at a reformatory for girls aged 14 to 18. Many of these girls had been juvenile delinquents for years, but a large number were girls from small villages, whose autocratic parents couldn't understand their new behavior patterns, and who had been sent to this reformatory for some minor misdemeanor.

Autocratic Tradition

A crisis situation had developed at this reformatory because of a change in administration. The new director, who had been exposed to Adlerian philosophy and wanted to experiment with some different methods, couldn't establish a leadership role with the former staff who wanted to maintain the previous pattern. There was also a great deal of antagonism between the existing staff and the girls.

Misguided Help

The situation was further exacerbated by the volunteers who had been brought in by the well intentioned Greek Adlerian Society, to be big sisters to the girls, but who were intensely disliked by them. The girls bitterly resented their elegant clothing and affluent way of life, and perceived them as bountiful ladies bestowing small gifts to bribe them into better behavior. The volunteers were therefore very apprehensive about their role and really did nothing to ameliorate the situation.

An attempt had also been made to help the girls through art therapy. One of the members of the Society whom I had trained tried some of my techniques, but the girls were not interested and typically attended for only a few minutes. This woman wisely gave up the idea of art therapy and worked with the few girls who became interested in just painting and wanted to develop skill in putting something recognizable on paper. This was their idea of what art and beauty meant. She won over these girls so that they were at least willing to spend half an hour each day practicing how to paint.

Bringing Everyone Together

It was at this point that I was called in to see if I could do something about improving relationships between the director, staff, volunteers, and inmates. I refused to work separately with each group, as was suggested, and agreed to help only if I could work with representatives from each group working as one. In order to include everyone, I worked with three mixed groups each day.

I began by using anti-suggestion with the girls, verbalizing what I guessed to be their hidden reason, as I think Rudolf would have done. I said, "If I were you, I wouldn't stay here for this discussion at all. I'd be thinking, 'What does this old woman want? How can she possibly understand what's going on in our lives? She doesn't know what it's like to be a young person and have problems. She doesn't even know our language.' If I were in your place, I'd simply leave. I wouldn't waste my time listening to something in which I wasn't interested." To my amazement, none of the girls left. I went on to say, "Please, sit near the door so that you can leave any time you want to without disturbing the group. However, if you *do* want to disturb us, just scatter around the room and leave when you feel like it. It won't make any difference." It was largely due to the efforts already made by the art teacher that the group was at all receptive. A core group of girls had confidence in her and she worked with me as a translator.

My first project was the usual carousel. Those who responded negatively were the representatives from the staff. They didn't see that anything could be accomplished by working in a group with the inmates. They considered them the enemy, and thought the only way to treat them was to punish the girls when they didn't behave well and keep them strictly in line. They couldn't understand how working in a group and doing the carousel would have any effect on them or the girls or anyone in the room.

Changing the Hierarchy

After the first session of the carousel, I asked the group to respond by telling us how they felt about what happened and their reactions to changing places versus painting by themselves. The girls who had been learning how to paint all liked the idea of changing places, because they already knew

138

what to do and could fix up some of the paintings as they followed behind those who didn't know how to do anything. This put them in an unaccustomed position of superiority.

The volunteers reported a sense of restraint and tension during the activity because they were very much aware of their tenuous relationship with the inmates and were worried about painting something that would displease or upset them. Staff members saw some merit in changing places and relating with the volunteers because they felt on a more equal basis with them than the girls.

Increased Cooperation

In the next session I asked each inmate to select another, either a staff member or volunteer, to paint with on one piece of paper. I allowed them to talk to each other during the activity. When all were finished it was time to show the paintings to the group. Maria, an inmate, and Elena, a volunteer, were first. I asked Maria what she had learned about Elena.

"I always thought Elena was a very mean lady and avoided her, but now I know she's not mean at all."

"How did you come to this conclusion?"

"Elena kept asking me what we should paint. No one has ever asked me what I wanted before. I was always told what to do. If Elena asked me for my opinion she can't be as mean as she looks."

"Was there anything else she did?"

"She painted a fence which looked like a prison window, and when I told her I didn't like to look out at bars she said, 'Please, Maria, paint it out. Paint anything you want there.' When she did that I realized that she's really a kind lady."

At this point Elena began to cry. "I didn't know I looked mean," she said. "Don't you know how you scared me? You ran away from me whenever I came near you and I never knew why until now. I don't want to look mean. I'll have to do something about it."

Maria put her arms around Elena and said, "I won't run away from you any more. Let's see if we can be friends." This theme was repeated in a variety of ways as each couple experienced a different reaction to the other while painting together.

The Magic Pill

The activity which proved to be most effective in establishing better relationships between all three groups was the "magic pill"* exercise. I actually walked around the room and pretended to put a pill in each of their mouths as I directed them to paint a picture of where they would like to be if magically transported to the place of their desire.

I chose one girl, one volunteer, and one staff person to put their paintings on the wall and talk about them. In this way each set of three discovered their commonality. What occurred when the first set described their paintings is a good example of this phenomenon.

The inmate had painted a broad field with a lake, sky, and mountains. She said, "I have just run away from this horrible place and the people who hurt me. I'm walking in the field and if anyone approaches me I'll jump in the lake. If they fish me out of the lake I'll climb the mountain so that no one can touch me or hurt me again. I don't want anything to do with people."

The staff member had painted a little house with a minibus and a field of grain. "I am in my village with my family. I've run away from this horrible place where I have to work to support them. I'm in prison here as if I'd committed a crime."

The volunteer had painted the Alps with chair lifts going up. "I'm climbing to the highest point," she said. "I hate being here. I only come here for a little while because it makes me feel superior to others who don't help these girls. I'm a medical student and my grades are very poor, but at least I feel superior to others when I'm here."

---

*The "magic pill" is an adaptation of Rudolf Dreikurs' (1977) method for differentiating between an organic and functional symptom. The method makes use of the three life tasks proposed by Adler, "love," "work," "community" (Adler, 1958), and the two proposed by Dreikurs and Mosak, getting along with oneself" (Dreikurs and Mosak, 1967) and the "spiritual" task (Dreikurs and Mosak, 1967). The patient "takes" the magic pill and then reports how his/her life will be different without the symptom. The patient points to the life task which is being avoided, e.g., "If I didn't have these headaches I could get a job." Thy symptom excuses the patient from responsibility for that task for which he/she feels incapable.

Used here, the magic pill points to the area of life to be avoided, i.e., the institution, and dramatically points to the fairy land where life would be perfect if it were not for the reality of their present circumstances.

Shared Ambition

When I asked each of the three what they had in common, they recognized that they all wanted to escape to the freedom of the country and open spaces from their own perceived prison, because of misbehavior, the social situation, or overambition.

As each set of three understood their similarities, the entire group began to look upon each other in a different way. They became fellow human beings in a difficult situation, each suffering in her own way and trying to find a place for herself in this world.

Changed Behavior

When I was finished with this project at the reformatory and asked for feedback, it was clear that there was a sense of understanding among the three groups and a greater desire to work together. The most gratifying result for me was the decision of the staff members to work with small groups of inmates in the future rather than with individuals.

Demonstrative Caring

I have two very sentimental memories associated with this project. The girls knit a scarf for me, each one knitting one inch. They chose the colors of the clothing I had worn during the sessions. When they gave it to me they said, "We're giving this to you so that when you feel cold you can put it around your neck and pretend we are hugging you."

I hesitate to report the other incident because it sounds like boasting, but it affected me deeply and indicated the potential for changes at that institution because of the general shift in attitude. One girl said to me, "I can't tell you what I've learned, but I want to ask you a question. Do you think you can come and live in Athens?"

"No. Why do you want me to live here?" I asked.

"We think that if you would live here and be our grandmother, we would not be bad girls any more."

Editorial Conclusion

In Rudolf Dreikurs' book *Social Equality: The Challenge of Today* (Dreikurs, 1971) he stated that we may call the present era the time of anxiety, the atomic era; but we are really in the beginning of the democratic era. In the few years since Rudolf Dreikurs wrote that comment, the world has changed dramatically.

Electro-tech Era

We are now in the electro-tech era. All of us are moving at a pace and knowledge level change not heretofore conceivable, but we are still in the beginning stages of democracy. The skills which Dreikurs described in 1971 to help us live as equals lest we destroy each other are today even more urgently needed.

Sadie Dreikurs

Sadie (Tee) Dreikurs has given us invaluable methods for promoting social equality. These methods can be used with extremely discouraged hospitalized patients, normal and disturbed individuals, or the staff of businesses or social organizations. They teach through participation the methods of social cooperation. Tee Dreikurs' approach to therapy is very positive. This method promotes social interest by releasing people from their fear of failure. It allows the creative self within each of us to overcome self-doubt and previous faulty education.

The typical education in the home and school occludes our creativity and plays down cooperation with others in favor of personal glory and superiority. This promotes a society of fear and competition. Tee's own experience with our discouraging methods of education might well have blocked forever a less courageous person. Through her own creativity, subsequent education, and friendships, Tee was able to revive the truth which she originally knew, "Cows can be purple."

142

Helping Others

Tee's return to faith in her own unique creativity is now skillfully used by her to help others express their uniqueness in a manner that does not block but promotes encouragement and social interest. An example of this approach which is typical of her style is seen in her comment to a rebellious individual: "Don't stifle your rebellion. Let is blossom. You have a unique contribution to make to others. No one else sees the world as you do. No one else has the ability to solve problems in the manner in which you see solutions." This is said to an individual who has felt only demands from others that he or she change and conform in order to be accepted. Tee's comments are extremely encouraging, and they are perhaps the first positive recognition that this discouraged person has felt. Such comments allow people to maintain their uniqueness, be accepted as they are, and to see possibilities for helping others and becoming willing contributors to the social group without having to conform to a conceived norm.

Confronting Discouragement

Tee knows that the root of inadequate functioning or maladjustment is discouragement. Therefore, she has designed her art therapy methods to expose people to positive experiences, as this is vital to overcoming the hesitating approach to life's tasks.

The hesitation which we all demonstrate when we feel unprepared for the task before us is evidence of our self-estimating, our continual desire to be above others. Because of our fear of being inferior we try to gain superiority over others. As Dreikurs stated, "Man is no longer a servant; he is the master of himself. But unaccustomed to his new role in society, man does not sense his mastery. He has not yet become aware of either his potentialities or his actual strength. Nor does he recognize the status as a social equal that a democratic society bestows upon him" (Dreikurs, 1971, p. xiv). Tee's art therapy exercises emphasize shared responsibility. This enhances the participants' positive feelings about themselves as it promotes social equality.

Shared Responsibility

Since we have not previously learned to live as social equals, we still feel like failures when we do not make it to the top, when we are not ahead of all others. Our faulty education results in our self-denegration when we are anything but number one. Tee Dreikurs dramatically demonstrates, often within a few minutes, that success has nothing to do with being first, winning or losing, or in any other way comparing oneself with others. Shared responsibility teaches cooperation and positive possibilities when the person becomes a contributing member of the art therapy group. Yet there is no threat to one's sense of individuality.

The Human Community

Again quoting from Dreikurs: "We need each other to remind us of our ideals and to give us persistence in pursuing them. We need each other to stimulate our devotion to the common good, to stir up our willingness to feel with each other, to live with each other, to belong to each other in a long-delayed fulfillment of humanity's most cherished and ancient dream: the brotherhood of man" (Dreikurs, 1971, p. 222). Tee's Adlerian philosophy and detailed methods of psychology which she has illustrated heuristically through her art therapy text, *Cows Can Be Purple,* can greatly assist us in achieving the ideals of which Dreikurs wrote so eloquently.

References

Adler, A. *The Case of Mrs. A.* Chicago: The Alfred Adler Institute, 1969.

Adler, A. *Problems of Neurosis; a Book of Case-Histories.* London: Kegan Paul, Trench, Truebnew & Co., 1929; reprinted, Chicago: Henry Regnery, 1970.

Adler, A. *The Science of Living.* New York: Greenberg, Publisher, 1929; reprinted, Garden City, N.Y.; Doubleday Anchor Books, 1969.

Adler, A. *What Life Should Mean to You.* Ed A. Porter. Boston: Little, Brown, 1951; reprinted, New York: Putnam Capricorn Books, 1958.

Dreikurs, R. "The Adlerian approach to therapy." In *Contemporary Psychotherapies*, ed. Morris L. Stein. New York: Free Press of Glencoe, 1961, pp. 80-94.

Dreikurs, R. *Group Psychotherapy and Group Approaches: Collected Papers.* Chicago: Alfred Adler Institute, 1960.

Dreikurs, R. Holistic medicine and the function of neurosis. *The Journal of Individual Psychology, 33,* 171-192.

Dreikurs, R. *Manual of Child Guidance.* Chicago: Chicago Medical School, 1945.

Dreikurs, R. *Psychodynamics, Psychotherapy, and Counseling: Collected Papers.* Chicago: Alfred Adler Institute, 1967.

Dreikurs, R. *Social Equality: The Challenge of Today.* Chicago: Henry Regnery Company, 1971, reprinted Chicago: The Alfred Adler Institute, 1984.

Dreikurs, R. Social interest: The basis of normalcy. *Counseling Psychologist,* 1969, 1:45-48.

Dreikurs, R., Corsini, R., Lowe, R., and Sonstegard, M. *Adlerian Family Counseling: A Manual for Counseling Centers.* Eugene, Ore.: University of Oregon Press, 1959.

Dreikurs, R., and Dinkmeyer, D. *Encouraging Children to Learn: The Encouragement Process.* Englewood Cliffs, N.J.: Prentice Hall, 1963.

Dreikurs, R., Grunwald, B. B., and Pepper, F. *Maintaining Sanity in the Classroom: Illustrated Teaching Techniques.* New York: Harper & Row, 1971.

Dreikurs, R., and Mosak, H. The tasks of life. II. The fourth life task. *Individual Psychologist,* 1967, 4:51-56.

145

Dreikurs, R., and Mosak, H. The tasks of life. III. The fifth life task. *Individual Psychologist,* 1967, 5:16.22.

Hall, C. S., and Lindzey, G. *Theories of Personality.* New York: Wiley, 1957.